# *SNAP!*

# *SNAP!*

## CHANGE YOUR PERSONALITY IN 30 DAYS

## GARY SMALL, MD, AND GIGI VORGAN

**Humanix Books**

www.humanixbooks.com

Humanix Books

SNAP!: Change Your Personality in 30 Days to Remake Yourself
Copyright © 2018 by Humanix Books
All rights reserved

Humanix Books, P.O. Box 20989, West Palm Beach, FL 33416, USA
www.humanixbooks.com | info@humanixbooks.com

Library of Congress Catalog-in-Publication data is available upon request.

Interior Design: Scribe Inc.

Humanix Books is a division of Humanix Publishing, LLC. Its trademark, consisting of the word "Humanix," is registered in the Patent and Trademark Office and in other countries.

Disclaimer: The information presented in this book is not specific medical advice for any individual and should not substitute medical advice from a health professional. If you have (or think you may have) a medical problem, speak to your doctor or a health professional immediately about your risk and possible treatments. Do not engage in any care of treatment without consulting a medical professional.

ISBN: 978-1-63006-091-6 (Hard Cover)
ISBN: 978-1-63006-092-3 (E-book)

*Printed in the United States of America*
10 9 8 7 6 5 4 3 2 1

# Contents

---

# Acknowledgments

---

**W**E ARE GRATEFUL TO the many volunteers and patients who participated in the research studies that inspired this book as well as the talented investigators who performed the studies. Thank you to our colleagues, friends, and family members who provided their guidance and input, including Howard Chang, Stuart and Valerie Grant, Rachel Small, and Harrison Small. Special thanks to our longtime agent and good friend, Sandra Dijkstra, as well as Mary Glenn at Humanix Books and Chris Ruddy at Newsmax Media.

Gary Small, MD, and Gigi Vorgan

*Note:* Many stories and examples contained in this book are composite accounts based on the experiences of several individuals and do not represent any one person or group of people. Similarities to any one person or persons are coincidental and unintentional. Readers may wish to talk with their doctor before starting any exercise or diet program.

# Preface

---

THINK OF A PERSON you admire. How would you describe her personality? Is she outgoing, warm, or conscientious? Do you think of her as funny, confident, or generous? Perhaps you wish you were more like her in some ways.

Consider someone you don't care for. What is it about his personality that bugs you? Is he anxious, short-tempered, or unreliable? You probably don't try to emulate that person.

Now describe your own personality. Are you extroverted and popular? Would you say you are efficient and organized? High strung or moody? Are there any qualities about yourself you would change if you could? If your answer is yes, you are not alone. Research shows that the vast majority of people do want to alter certain aspects of their personality, and not just a little bit. Most desire profound personal improvements but don't even know that change is possible.

Personality defines who we are as individuals. It is a sum of the relatively stable traits that make up our unique character and is driven by our distinctive patterns of thoughts, feelings, and behaviors. Each of us has a personality fingerprint that reflects who we are—our inner temperament that drives how we act and react in the world.

Experts in psychiatry and psychology have long believed that our personalities are essentially set from early childhood and remain consistent throughout life. However, the latest scientific evidence contradicts this long-held assumption. New compelling evidence indicates that we *can* change our personalities (either on our own, with the help of a therapist, or a combination of the two) and meaningful personality change can be achieved in a *snap*—as little as 30 days. These groundbreaking findings have shattered the false belief that we are locked into our negative personality traits, no matter how much they hinder our potential happiness and success.

As you read *SNAP!*, you will gain a better understanding of who you are now, how others see you, and which aspects of yourself you'd like to change. You will acquire the tools you need to change your personality in just one month—it won't take years of psychotherapy, self-exploration, or rehashing every single bad thing that's ever happened to you. If you are committed to change, this book will provide a road map to achieving your goals and becoming a better you.

Gary Small, MD
Gigi Vorgan
Los Angeles, CA

# CHAPTER 1

## Personality Can Change

*People always ask me, "Were you funny as a child?" Well, no, I was an accountant.*

—Ellen DeGeneres

**E**MMA FINALLY MADE IT to the front of the line at the bar and ordered a white wine. She had to yell because the band was playing too loud. She hated weddings, especially when she had to come alone. At 35, her parents and friends were starting to give up on her ever getting married. They accused her of being too choosy, but Emma knew that it was really just her shyness that always got in the way of making romantic connections.

She took a seat at table 12, her designated torture chair for the evening, and began calculating just how early she could make an escape. A couple of giggly women sat down and introduced themselves, but Emma couldn't hear them over the band's rendition of "New York, New York."

After the toasts and before the salad, an attractive man from the next table came over and sat next to Emma. He said hello and asked her to dance. Emma avoided his eyes and shook her head. He turned and asked one of the gigglers instead. As Emma watched them walk to the dance floor, her inner voice screamed, *What is your problem? He was cute and you are an idiot.* Then she calmed herself by repeating her mantra of late: *Forget about it; he was probably married or a jerk anyway.*

Emma reached for her third dinner roll, but there was no more butter. She grumbled to herself, *I should have stayed home.*

Emma is one of the millions of people who suffer from excessive shyness and insecurity. She knew this about herself and accepted her fate. Sure, she would have liked to be more extroverted and open to new things, but that just wasn't the personality she was dealt.

The term *personality* is derived from the Latin word *persona*, which refers to the theatrical masks worn by actors to display various roles or to hide their true identities. Today we think of personality as incorporating an individual's characteristic patterns of thoughts, feelings, and behaviors. How we feel and think drives our behavior and causes us to act in certain ways.

Your personality traits tend to remain consistent over the years, and they have a major impact on your love life, career success, health outcomes, and even life expectancy. And although some of us may act in similar ways, no two people share the exact same character style.

Most people have a pretty good sense of who they are—they know themselves to be a certain way and behave accordingly. If you consider yourself to be creative, you probably do original things. If you think of yourself as generous, you are likely to be a giving person. If you believe you are overly sensitive, you probably get your feelings hurt a lot.

Sometimes it's easier to identify the personality traits of other people than it is to accurately describe yourself. Think of a few people you know, perhaps siblings, friends, or work associates. You may be able to sum up their personalities in one word: Jim is bossy; Carol is intellectual; Sharon is temperamental;

Peter is conscientious. Of course, one word is insufficient to define a whole person, but we tend to use these labels as shortcuts to determine how we will respond and act toward others.

## TRAITS VERSUS STATES

When we refer to someone's personality *traits*, we usually mean the consistent emotions and behavior patterns they display over time (e.g., generosity, moodiness, shyness). By contrast, emotional *states* stem from more transient thoughts and feelings that drive our behaviors, often in response to external stimuli. For example, your brother may be a basically cheerful person, but if faced with a major loss or disappointment, he might become depressed for a while. His depressed mood would be a temporary *state* he is experiencing due to his current situation.

My patient Frank, a single father, was a self-described worrywart. Even when his life was going well, Frank would obsess over what might go wrong next. When his son was in elementary school, Frank worried about getting the car pool to school on time. When his son got a driver's license, he fretted about the boy getting into an accident. Frank's anxiety levels were certainly elevated compared with a person who was less neurotic, but they didn't change that much from day to day. Worrying was one of Frank's lifelong consistent *traits*.

Eventually Frank's son did have a car accident, although no one was seriously hurt. When Frank received the call, his anxiety escalated to the point that he couldn't catch his breath and he thought he was having a heart attack. After a normal cardiogram in the emergency room, the doctor diagnosed the episode as a panic attack with hyperventilation. Frank took a mild tranquilizer, breathed into a paper bag, and was able to calm down. His panic attack was a temporary emotional *state*—a reaction to

an upsetting incident—and was not a regular *trait* or characteristic of his personality.

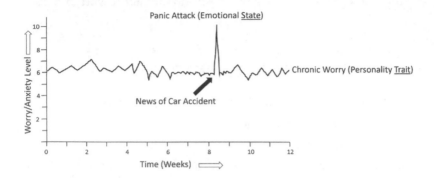

## HOW PERSONALITY IS FORMED

Doctors and other experts have long theorized that our personalities are formed in early childhood and remain consistent
throughout life. Research has suggested that by first grade, children have already developed personality traits that can predict
their adult behavior.

When I began to study psychiatry, I delved deeper into various
theories of personality formation. Sigmund Freud speculated
that each child progresses through different stages of psycho-
sexual development, which shape that person's long-term dis-
position. Erik Erickson described eight stages of developmental
crises that mold personality. He speculated that an individual's
insecurity stemmed from an impasse during one of those eight
stages, such as young adulthood, when struggles with intimacy
versus isolation are common. Behaviorists like B. F. Skinner
and John Watson held that personality stems from interactions
between the individual and the environment. Carl Rogers, Abra-
ham Maslow, and other humanist theorists emphasized free will
and experience as the driving forces that form personality.

John Bowlby theorized that an infant's early attachment or
basic need for closeness with their first caregiver (usually the

mother) was the basis for that child's long-term adaptive strategies to relationships, which can influence personality traits. Bowlby posited that a baby who received caring and consistent parenting early in life would form a secure attachment and grow to be an independent, self-reliant, and curious person. However, infants who don't form a secure attachment may become needy, insecure, and distrustful of others and may have difficulty making friends.

During my psychiatry training, I found these and other theories to be interesting, but I conjectured that a person's early life experiences could not be the whole story. Even though I was taught to understand personality at a psychological level, I presumed that genetics must come in to play. Studies have shown that identical twins who share 100 percent of the same DNA are significantly more likely to share personality traits than fraternal twins who share only 50 percent of their DNA. This early work and later studies made clear that our genes do affect our personalities. However, the relationship is complex, and no specific personality gene has yet been discovered.

Research indicates that the heritability of our personalities—or what proportion of our character is inherited from our parents—varies from about 40 to 60 percent depending on the particular personality trait being considered. That means that for the average person, about 50 percent of what determines their personalities is *not* genetic—each of us may have much more control over our personalities than we realize.

## WHAT IS PERSONALITY?

If you think about the various people in your life, you can probably come up with several different adjectives to describe their personalities—both positive and negative—including the ones below:

## COMMON PERSONALITY TRAITS

| Positive | Negative |
| --- | --- |
| Bold | Timid |
| Calm | Short-tempered |
| Flexible | Rigid |
| Funny | Humorless |
| Generous | Self-centered |
| Modest | Arrogant |
| Outgoing | Shy |
| Trustworthy | Dishonest |

Of course, a generally positive trait can convert to a negative one if it becomes too extreme. A flexible person may be willing to compromise and get along with others, but being too flexible could make one indecisive and afraid to take a stand. Outgoing people tend to attract many friends, but some outgoing individuals go too far and become intrusive.

For years, psychologists have grappled with categorizing the various personality styles and traits that people exhibit. Using a statistical method known as factor analysis, researchers found that the multitude of descriptors for personality fell into five major groups. These findings were corroborated when four independent teams of investigators, using different methods, confirmed that almost all known personality traits can be organized into the following "Big Five" categories: extraversion, openness, emotional stability, agreeableness, and conscientiousness. Each person's personality consists of a combination of traits within these groupings, and the qualities shared within each category follow common themes:

- *Extraversion.* Extroverts are outgoing, have lots of energy, and tend to do well in social situations. You might describe them as assertive, bold, and talkative, but some may lack restraint and take unnecessary risks.

- *Openness.* People who are open like adventure, seek novelty, and welcome challenges. They are creative, bright, and imaginative and enjoy intellectual stimulation.
- *Emotional stability.* People who are emotionally stable are calm, relaxed, and self-confident. This personality trait is the antithesis of the moody, high-strung, and temperamental features of neuroticism.
- *Agreeableness.* Agreeable people are friendly, sympathetic, and warm. They are pleasant to be around and are considerate of other people's feelings. However, if someone is too agreeable, they may be taken advantage of.
- *Conscientiousness.* Conscientious people are masters of self-control and efficiency. They tend to be neat and organized, and they are careful when making decisions. They can be counted on to get the job done, although too much conscientiousness can lead to obsessive-compulsive behaviors.

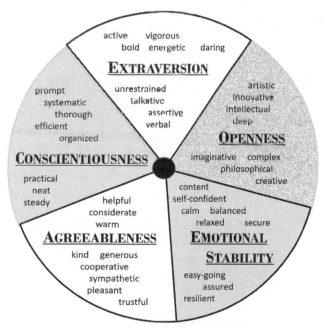

## BIG FIVE PERSONALITY WHEEL

Our individuality is determined by where we fall on the spectrum within each of these five personality categories. For example, if you are an extremely popular person, you would probably
score high on a measure of extraversion. If you tend to ruminate
and neurotically obsess over things, you would likely score low
on an emotional stability scale.

Consider Emma at the wedding. If we describe her personality
based solely on her experience on that particular day, she would
score pretty low on an extraversion rating. She also didn't seem
very open to new experiences, so she would score low on openness. She kept second-guessing herself and putting herself down
for her choices, indicating that she would rank fairly low on the
emotional stability scale. Emma was curt to the man who asked
her to dance, which would lower her score on the agreeableness
scale. She did, however, show up at her friend's wedding instead
of skipping it, which raised her conscientiousness rating.

If we were to rate Emma's Big Five personality traits on a scale
from one to five, her scores might chart like this:

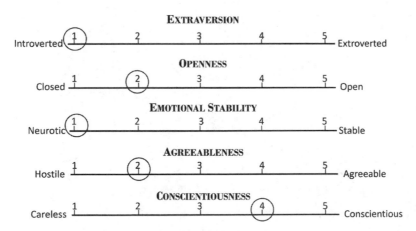

Keep in mind that we are basing this assessment on one brief vignette from Emma's life. If we got to know her better, we might learn that she volunteers regularly at the women's shelter. That compassionate characteristic would raise her agreeableness rating. And although she was emotionally closed off at the wedding, at other times she may enjoy creative pursuits like dancing or studying art history, which raises her openness rating. Clearly, the better we get to know people, the more accurately we can describe their personalities. This holds true for ourselves as well. The better we understand our own personalities, the easier it will be to focus on what we want to change and how to do it.

Our brain structure actually varies depending on our personality style. At the University of Minnesota, Colin DeYoung and his coworkers assessed the personalities of 116 volunteers ages 18 to 40 (22 years old on average) and performed magnetic resonance imaging (MRI) brain scans to determine the relative sizes of their different brain regions. The scientists' findings, published in the journal *Psychological Science*, indicated that the medial orbitofrontal cortex, a brain region just behind and above the eyes, was significantly larger in extroverts compared with introverts. This is not surprising since this region controls the brain's reward system—extroverts seek more positive experiences through social interactions and the pursuit of excitement and adventure. Volunteers who were more conscientious showed larger volumes in the lateral prefrontal cortex, which controls a person's ability to plan ahead. In neurotic study subjects, brain volume was larger in a nearby region, the dorsomedial prefrontal cortex, and in an area under the temples that controls emotional reactions, the medial temporal lobe.

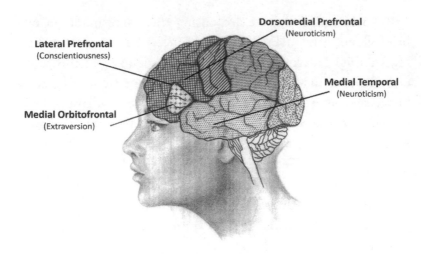

**Dorsomedial Prefrontal**
(Neuroticism)

**Lateral Prefrontal**
(Conscientiousness)

**Medial Temporal**
(Neuroticism)

**Medial Orbitofrontal**
(Extraversion)

## PERSONALITY EXTREMES: WHEN TRAITS BECOME DISORDERS

Everyday life can be stressful, and most of us react to that stress with upsetting emotions like anxiety, sadness, or anger. Although these feelings are usually short-lived, some people experience these types of emotions chronically, and that can become a problem.

Sometimes personality traits and their accompanying behavior patterns become so extreme that they impair an individual's success and ability to function normally. In fact, when *any* mental condition becomes so severe that it disrupts a person's life, it is considered a *disorder.*

Personality disorders are essentially character traits taken to the extreme. If a patient's desire for orderliness becomes excessive and interferes with their ability to work, they may fall out of the conscientious personality category and meet the diagnostic criteria for obsessive-compulsive *disorder.* Think of how shy Emma was at the wedding. If her shyness grew more extreme to the point that she isolated herself and rarely connected with other people, that personality trait might become a phobic disorder.

Those who suffer from personality disorders can cause others around them to feel uncomfortable. In response to this discomfort, many people employ personality-disorder terminology to label and disparage those with disorders: Lily is such a narcissist—she only cares about herself. Fred's a pathological liar and can't be trusted. Lois thinks everyone's out to get her—she's so paranoid. Although labeling may temporarily reduce the anxiety many people feel about those with difficult personalities, it doesn't provide any real insight into their behavior, and it comes at the expense of their empathy.

---

## MAJOR PERSONALITY DISORDERS

The American Psychiatric Association's *Diagnostic and Statistical Manual of Mental Disorders* (fifth edition) lists the following personality disorders that cause social and professional impairment:

- *Antisocial.* People with this disorder lack empathy, cannot distinguish right from wrong, persistently lie and exploit others, and use their charm to manipulate others for personal gain. They often have legal problems, take unnecessary risks, and engage in abusive relationships.

- *Avoidant.* These individuals suffer from feelings of social inadequacy and inhibition; they are extremely sensitive to any criticism or rejection and have major difficulties interacting with others and maintaining relationships.

- *Borderline.* These patients live in a world that borders between typical neurotic behavior and full-blown psychosis wherein they lose touch with reality. They have a disturbed sense of identity and are sensitive to real or imagined abandonment. They are impulsive and have intense, uncontrollable emotional outbursts. Their relationships are chaotic, and they often suffer from depression, psychosis, substance abuse, and suicidal behavior.

- *Obsessive-compulsive*. People with an obsessive-compulsive disorder are preoccupied by rules and details. Extreme perfectionists, they become distressed when they fall short of their ideals. They try to control others and have trouble delegating tasks. They are rigid, stubborn, and have trouble letting go of worthless objects.

- *Narcissistic*. These self-centered individuals often have unrealistic fantasies about the extent of their power, success, and attractiveness. They come off as arrogant, lack empathy, and frequently take advantage of others. They exaggerate their own achievements and seek constant praise and admiration.

- *Schizotypal*. These patients usually appear peculiar in their dress, thinking, beliefs, and behavior. They may hear voices whispering to them and experience other odd perceptions. Many engage in "magical thinking," wherein they believe that their inner feelings, thoughts, or desires can affect the external world. They are often uncomfortable with close relationships and can be suspicious of others.

## THE SLOW LANE OF PERSONALITY CHANGE

Thankfully, less than 10 percent of the population suffers from a true personality disorder that debilitates their lives. However, the other 90 percent of us are not necessarily happy with each and every aspect of our own personalities. Many of the patients I see believe that one or more of their character traits are holding them back from reaching their professional goals, forming satisfying and supportive relationships, and remaining mentally and physically healthy. And for the longest time, there didn't seem like much we could do about it, outside of the slow and laborious changes that can sometimes be achieved through psychoanalysis.

Psychoanalysis is a branch of psychiatry and psychology that has been successful in helping some patients with personality traits that disrupt their lives. It involves intensive, long-term treatment approaches and can also help some patients with borderline, narcissistic, or other personality disorders. In Freudian psychoanalysis, a patient with problems or mental symptoms verbalizes their free associations, fantasies, and dreams to the analyst. The analyst then interprets the unconscious conflicts that are thought to cause the patient's issues. Once the patient gains insight from the analyst's interpretations, the symptoms often improve, but it can take years of nearly daily treatment, which is expensive and obviously very time consuming. Also, controlled systematic trials proving the effectiveness of psychoanalysis in altering personality traits are limited.

## NEW RESEARCH TURNS PERSONALITY SCIENCE UPSIDE DOWN

If you've known someone for a long time, you may have noticed that certain aspects of his personality have gotten mellower with age. Real-life experiences and milestones—like becoming a first-time parent—may have altered his perspective and made him more conscientious in order to meet his new responsibilities. Perhaps with age he began to worry less about peer pressure or future events going wrong. Studies have shown that these gradual and modest changes happen throughout life. Whether they occur in young adulthood, middle age, or even late in life, they tend to soften us. Over time, we do gradually become more agreeable, confident, conscientious, and stable. And although this can be an upside of aging, the degree of change is very modest and it takes decades to occur.

## HOW DO YOU PERCEIVE YOUR OWN PERSONALITY?

Place a number between 1 (strongly disagree) and 10 (strongly agree) for each of the following statements to quickly see how you rate your own personality on the Big Five Inventory. The higher your score, the stronger your personality trait.

| Personality Domain | Statement | Your Score |
|---|---|---|
| Extraversion | I am outgoing and assertive. | |
| Openness | I am creative and adventurous. | |
| Emotional stability | I am self-confident and easygoing. | |
| Agreeableness | I am supportive and cooperative. | |
| Conscientiousness | I am organized and focused. | |

In a 40-year study, investigators assessed personality traits in elementary school students and then reassessed those volunteers four decades later. They found remarkable consistency in the volunteers' personalities: impulsive kids remained impetuous as adults, and agreeable youngsters were still cooperative decades later. A limitation of this and many other studies was that researchers were tracking personality traits in people who never received any psychological treatment or used any self-help strategies.

Based on all available research to date, most psychiatrists, including myself, have been trained to operate under the assumption that true core personality traits are fundamentally set by early childhood. In therapy, we could help patients change specific behaviors but not necessarily the basics of their personalities.

But now, startling new research contradicts that long-held tenet. The latest science points to a new conclusion that has literally reversed our assumptions about how—and how rapidly—personality can change. To explore whether it's possible for personality traits to change quickly through interventions like therapy and just how rapidly such change could occur, psychologist Brent Roberts and his coworkers at the University of Illinois did an in-depth assessment of hundreds of studies looking at assorted types of treatments.

This approach to answering a scientific question is called meta-analysis, which uses statistical methods to combine the results of multiple scientific studies. The statistical methods pool estimates from the various studies to reach a conclusion that is valid. Many investigators consider meta-analysis to be one of the most robust forms of scientific evidence, but it is essential for the investigators to choose the right studies to include.

---

### DID YOU KNOW?

- Although firstborn children tend to score higher on intelligence tests, birth order has no influence on self-reported personality traits.

- People who identify themselves as dog lovers tend to be more extroverted, while those who consider themselves cat people tend to be more introverted.

---

Plenty of psychological and mental health studies have demonstrated that certain forms of psychotherapy or medication treatment can benefit a range of mental states such as depressive episodes, panic attacks, or psychotic breaks. However, relatively few studies have targeted stable personality traits like conscientiousness or agreeableness. The researchers at the University of Illinois included only well-controlled investigations that specifically focused on measures of personality as outcomes of the interventions.

They systematically searched for the best-controlled studies that asked whether different interventions changed personality. The scientists searched for not only studies of therapies involving mental health professionals but self-help strategies as well. They wanted to include investigations and interventions that used control groups (i.e., volunteers who received no interventions at all) because patients often respond well to an inactive placebo treatment or by simply getting on a waiting list to receive a treatment. Those nonspecific influences on personality change needed to be factored out of the equation.

After an extensive search, they identified more than 200 studies that were of high enough quality to include in the meta-analysis. Each of the studies contained enough subjects to draw meaningful conclusions. And they all assessed one or more of the Big Five personality categories as outcome measures.

The number of volunteers totaled more than 20,000. Study subjects were mostly women (63 percent) and ranged in age from 19 to 73 years (on average, 36 years). Although personality change was the focus of the new meta-analysis, many of the research subjects were being treated for other mental conditions such as anxiety, depression, or substance abuse, while others had no specific mental disorder during the course of the study. Interventions also varied from medication treatments to various forms of psychotherapy and self-help approaches. Many of the interventions consisted of one-on-one therapies, while others involved group treatments or do-it-yourself methods.

---

**TYPES OF INTERVENTIONS THAT CAN CHANGE PERSONALITY**

- Cognitive behavioral therapy

- Mindfulness intervention

- Psychoanalytic/psychodynamic therapy

- Psychopharmacological treatment

- Relaxation training

- Social skill training

- Supportive psychotherapy

---

Because the various studies and types of interventions differed, the researchers needed to use a measure that would level the playing field in order to make their comparisons. They employed a statistical calculation known as the *effect size* to compare the benefits of all the various interventions. The effect size is essentially a number from 0 to 1 that indicates how much more effective a treatment is in a group of subjects when compared to a control group receiving placebo or no treatment at all. An effect size of 0.2 or less is considered small; the 0.3 to 0.5 range is thought of as medium; and anything at 0.6 or above is categorized as a large effect.

When the scientists systematically pooled all the results from this large meta-analysis, they drew a remarkable conclusion: both clinical (involving treatment from a mental health professional) and nonclinical self-help interventions (such as internet-based cognitive therapy or meditation) resulted in positive improvements in personality traits over a relatively brief period of time. Also, for the subjects who were followed a year or more after the treatment was completed, researchers found that the personality benefits resulting from the interventions were sustained.

The type of therapy didn't seem to matter much when it came to improving personality traits in the subjects. Supportive psychotherapy, psychodynamic therapy, and cognitive behavior therapy demonstrated comparable levels of benefits, while hospitalization and psychopharmacology were only slightly less effective. Whether or not the research volunteers were being treated for depression, anxiety, or no particular disorder at all also had no influence on the results: personality traits consistently improved in the full range of people who were studied.

Some personality traits were more sensitive to treatment than were others. The greatest personality changes were observed for emotional stability followed by extraversion, agreeableness, conscientiousness, and openness.

## HOW FAST CAN CHANGE HAPPEN?

Professor Roberts and his colleagues assumed that very short interventions would not do much to change personality—they expected that one hour, one day, or one week of intervention couldn't budge the long-term dispositions of the study subjects—so they also included studies that involved long-term therapies lasting many months.

To determine how long someone has to continue an intervention like therapy before it has a positive effect on personality, the researchers plotted each treatment's degree of impact according to its duration. When they charted the effect size versus the duration of a treatment, another unexpected discovery was revealed: Most positive changes in personality were achieved within the first month of therapy. After that, the rate of change leveled off and the benefits plateaued.

Additional treatment didn't provide any incremental improvement, but the original personality benefits achieved during the first 30 days remained stable and continued long after the treatment ended. The graph below shows the increase from neuroticism to emotional stability according to the number of weeks in treatment.

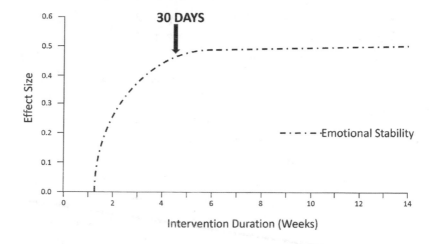

The surprising conclusion from this science is clear: We *can* change our personalities if we choose to, and meaningful change can be achieved as quickly as 30 days. Also, a variety of self-help therapies work, so meaningful personality improvements don't necessarily require the help of a trained professional.

## YOUR PERSONALITY IMPACTS YOUR LIFE

Some individuals readily accept who they are and how their life is going, good or bad. They have no desire or drive to change anything about themselves, especially their personality. Many people, however, feel that one or more of their character traits are holding them back—affecting their relationships, careers, and all-around life satisfaction. If you are someone who wishes to change, there is good reason to do so. Compelling scientific evidence indicates that your personality predicts many important outcomes in your life, including your physical health, success in relationships, and financial security.

Your personality traits also influence your life-span expectancy. Extroverts who tend to be friendlier and more socially connected enjoy greater longevity than introverts. People who are more neurotic have a shorter life expectancy than do more emotionally stable individuals. A large British study showed that cardiovascular illnesses contributed to the increased risk of death in neurotic people. Less conscientious people don't live as long as those who are more conscientious, and it's not surprising that those prone to taking risks may live more exciting lives, but on average their life-spans are shorter.

Your brain health and risk for several age-related illnesses can be affected by your personality style. Developing memory loss is one of the greatest concerns that people have as they age, and when that memory loss interferes with an individual's independence, it is called dementia. We know that healthy lifestyle strategies—exercising regularly, eating right, managing stress, and remaining social—can reduce the risk of dementia, but your personality style has an influence as well. Investigators at the Karolinska Institute in Stockholm, Sweden, assessed personality traits in more than 500 older adults without dementia and followed them on average for six years. High emotional stability in combination with high extraversion was the personality-trait pattern associated with the lowest risk of dementia as well as other mental disorders, such as major depression, substance abuse, and phobia. In socially isolated people, high emotional stability alone appeared to decrease the risk for cognitive decline.

Having high ratings on the conscientiousness scale predicts several significant life outcomes. A National Institute on Aging study published in the *Journal of Economic Psychology* showed that a person's degree of conscientiousness has a major influence on career success. Other investigations indicate that higher degrees of conscientiousness are associated with higher income levels, regardless of an individual's type of work. That trait also predicts the duration and happiness of a person's marriage. And

---

**PERSONALITY TRAITS OF STAND-UP COMEDIANS**

Stand-up comedians are very creative individuals who write and perform their material and either enjoy or suffer from immediate audience feedback. In contrast to actors, stand-ups tend to score high on disagreeableness, which may account for the disparaging humor of many. Although they don't appear to be any more neurotic than people in the general population, they tend to be more introverted.

---

because conscientious people are more fastidious about their health care, they not only live longer; they also are less likely to suffer a stroke, develop high blood pressure, or get Alzheimer's disease. Those better outcomes could in part reflect a conscientious person's tendency to not smoke, avoid drinking alcohol in excess, and follow up on medical advice.

Many explanations contribute to these varied outcomes of an individual's personality style. Neurotic people don't handle stress well, and chronic stress can lead to depression, age-related physical illnesses, accidents, and other outcomes that make for a briefer life-span. They also don't take care of their health as well as more emotionally stable individuals. By contrast, a friendly extrovert enjoys the support of a social network that can lend a hand when that person becomes ill or stressed out.

The bottom line is that we are no longer prisoners of our old personality traits. If we make the decision to free ourselves from those traits that hold us back, we can begin to achieve the life we want.

## WHEN IS THE BEST TIME TO CHANGE?

The simple, concise answer to this question is right now. Because most people find comfort in their routines, even when those routines disrupt their lives and hold them back from their goals, it can be difficult to initiate change. Getting started is often the most challenging step.

Keep in mind that just *trying* to change your personality can take forever, but *committing* to change and making it happen is within your reach—and it can happen in only 30 days. By picking up this book, you have already taken your first step. Whether you opt to work with a therapist, employ self-help strategies, or both, the following chapters will provide you with a road map for becoming a better you.

# CHAPTER 2

---

# Four Phases of Change

---

*When people are ready to, they change. They
never do it before then.*

—Andy Warhol

**A**T SOME POINT IN life, almost everyone has something about
themselves they would like to change, whether it's improving
their relationships, advancing their career, losing weight, or just
becoming more relaxed and mindful. Some fortunate individuals are able to easily define a goal, get started, and achieve the
change they desire. However, most people have a hard enough
time figuring out what needs to change, let alone knowing how
to get there. That is why it's important to learn strategies that
can help you move smoothly through the process.

As a psychiatrist, I have helped many patients change their personalities through psychotherapy, and I know that the patient's
motivation is a critical component for success. But even the most
motivated patients may still need to overcome certain obstacles
before they can truly alter their lives for the better.

During the past several decades, an emerging science of
behavior change has systematically helped many people reach

their goals. These methods challenge one's previously failed change strategies and help remove the roadblocks that interfere with personal growth and achieving specific goals.

## WHAT IS CPAS?

How many times have you told yourself that you were going to drop those extra pounds? Or start being more patient with your teenagers? Perhaps you've been meaning to try meditation or join a gym, but you just haven't got around to it. It's easy to find reasons and excuses not to change, and unfortunately some people never become motivated to move beyond that point.

For those of us who are motivated, however, there is a critical moment when we shift from wishing we could change to actually doing something about it. That tipping point can be different for everyone, but once we reach it, the road to change becomes a true possibility.

Diane, a 28-year-old waitress, always had a bad temper. Growing up, her explosive outbursts got her into trouble at home and in school, but she felt justified in her anger because everybody else was usually wrong. Her parents couldn't change her, and in the past few years, she had alienated her now ex-husband and lost two jobs due to workplace altercations. When she finally got hired at another restaurant, she swore things would be different. But on the second day, she pissed off a regular customer who vowed never to return.

Diane got fired from the new job, and she could no longer deny that she wasn't at fault. She realized, deep down, that she had to make a change, but she had no idea how to go about it.

Behavioral psychologists have developed various theories in attempting to explain behavior change. For example, the *Fogg Behavior Model* posits that behavior change involves ability, motivation, and triggers. The *Health Belief Model* suggests that beliefs about threats to well-being and effectiveness, as well as outcomes of specific actions, will determine behaviors. The *Theory of Planned Behavior* proposes that an individual's behavior is proportional to the amount of control that they have over their own actions and the strength of their intentions. The *Transtheoretical Model* describes five stages a person must proceed through in order to achieve change.

These various models and theories are helpful in providing the framework for understanding the change process. To make them more practical, however, I have adapted these theories to create a more user-friendly approach for each individual to determine their readiness for change, formulate a plan, and achieve their goals.

This approach, which I call the **CPAS Method for Change**, stands for **c**onsidering, **p**lanning, **a**cting, and **s**ustaining new traits and habits—the sequence of phases that lead to meaningful personality change. It's easy for me to remember because it reminds me of my accountants who I meet with every April. With the right motivation, most people are able to move sequentially through these CPAS phases and achieve their objectives either on their own, with the help of a psychotherapist, or a combination of the two. This approach is effective for a variety of goals, including losing weight, improving relationships, or becoming more assertive.

My longtime friend Jackson had gradually put on pounds during his 30s and 40s and hadn't done any regular exercise since college. I was concerned because now that he was in his 50s, those extra pounds around the middle could increase his risk for Alzheimer's disease, diabetes, coronary disease, and other age-related illnesses. When I occasionally mentioned these issues, he would laugh it off or joke that he needed his belly to play Santa Claus for the kids. My invitations to go on a hike or meet at the gym fell on deaf ears. I considered gifting Jackson a couple of free sessions with my trainer, but I was concerned he might feel pressured, which could further discourage him from changing his behavior.

I knew that behind all the jokes, at an intellectual level, Jackson acknowledged the health benefits of exercise, but he wasn't motivated enough to begin considering a real change in his behavior. Ten months later Jackson suffered a mild heart attack. It scared him, and he was finally motivated enough to make a change and get in shape. This change benefitted his overall future health, because adopting one healthy habit often leads to others.

Once you are ready to commit to your CPAS Method for Change, you will already be in your planning phase and ready to choose whether you wish to work with a psychotherapist, self-help techniques, or both.

---

### CPAS–THE FOUR PHASES OF CHANGE

Whether you wish to change a specific behavior or alter an aspect of your personality, the same four phases apply, and they progress in the following order:

1. *Considering.* Your barriers and excuses for continuing an unwanted behavior or personality trait are no longer working. You are thinking about making a change, but you may still be ambivalent and not convinced that change is possible.

2. *Planning.* You have identified what you wish to change about yourself and you are highly motivated. You can now decide whether to move forward on your own, with the help of a therapist, or a combination of the two.

3. *Acting.* You have established your plan for change and are ready to act on it. You begin the process of adopting new behaviors and ways of thinking and giving up your old ways. Once people begin taking action, change can happen swiftly–in as little as 30 days.

4. *Sustaining.* Now that you have achieved the change you hoped for, you will learn strategies to sustain the new version of you over time.

## CONSIDERING

Someone in the considering phase is not quite ready to change or adopt new behaviors, but they are inching toward a state of readiness. At the beginning of this phase, people typically make excuses for keeping their lives at the status quo: "I don't really need that many friends; I'm fine on my own" or "I know I'm constantly late for things, but my dad was like that too." When more closely examined, such excuses are merely a way of skirting the emotional work necessary to make a personality change.

At the beginning of the considering phase, many people already recognize that their behavior is a problem, but they don't think it's possible for them to change. When they envision altering their behaviors, it all seems too complicated or daunting. They aren't yet motivated enough to go for it; however, maintaining the status quo is no longer working in their lives.

When my neighbor Shirley was still in graduate school, she went to a therapist for her anxiety issues. However, the therapist kept delving into Shirley's early childhood, which made her feel even more anxious, so she gave up and assumed that no form of psychotherapy would ever help her.

Often someone's previous failed attempts at change can reinforce this kind of thinking. Shirley's first try at therapy failed, so she allowed that to become a barrier against any change at all. Individuals in the considering phase often create imagined barriers that serve as excuses to remain stuck in old, unproductive patterns.

Transitioning through this stage involves identifying strong motivators as well as pinpointing and overcoming one's barriers. Some people stay in the considering phase for long periods, remaining ambivalent about whether the effort is worth it to them, and they are not yet motivated enough to try.

It wasn't until recently that Shirley's escalating anxiety symptoms began affecting her health—her asthma was worsening and she was developing irritable bowel syndrome. Her declining health supplied the motivation she needed to make a change. She found a behavioral psychologist who did not delve into her childhood but instead focused on the here and now. This time therapy made Shirley feel better instead of worse, and she was able to discover the root of her anxiety and overcome it.

Connecting with other people who have made successful changes in their lives can also be very motivating. Many studies have shown that when we spend time with people who engage in healthy behaviors, we are more likely to engage in those behaviors ourselves. If your goal is to become more agreeable, hanging out with other agreeable people will no doubt help you achieve that goal.

Once my friend Jackson accepted that he needed to change his eating habits and start exercising, he entered the considering phase of change—not quite ready to meet me at the gym, but beginning to formulate a plan to move forward. I advise patients in this phase to begin thinking about small but achievable goals for themselves and to work on understanding the feelings behind their barriers to change.

## PLANNING

People in the planning phase have overcome their ambivalence; they know what they want to achieve and are sufficiently motivated. Many in this phase begin experimenting with various strategies, embracing some and discarding others.

To ensure progress through the planning phase, it's important to establish a concrete blueprint for change. Brainstorming with a therapist, friend, or family member can be helpful when deciding which strategies to try. Just the process of writing down several possible approaches can accelerate one's progression.

Jackson's busy work schedule made it impossible for him to get to the gym during the week, so he compiled a list of ways to squeeze in some cardiovascular conditioning every day at work. He started by taking the stairs instead of the elevator to his office on the eighth floor. Of course, he wasn't in good enough shape to climb all eight flights right away, so he began by climbing one flight up each day for the first week, two flights the next week, and so forth.

Ambivalence may still occur during the planning phase. Reviewing your reasons and motivators for change may assist you in getting to the bottom of your ambivalence and overcoming it. Understanding any lingering feelings that are causing resistance to change can help make your plans more concrete so you can move forward.

## CHANGING YOUR PERSONALITY ALTERS YOUR BRAIN

When we alter our personality, we also change our brain. For each phase of change, different brain regions become engaged and work together to solidify our new behaviors and traits. When practicing a new behavior, the *prefrontal cortex* (the thinking brain) sends signals to the *midbrain*, which then releases the "feel good" chemical messenger dopamine as a reward for the new, better behavior or personality trait. Another region, the *striatum*, coordinates these signals, and if the new trait doesn't pan out, dopamine declines, the behavior is less rewarding, and we are less likely to adopt it. However, if the new behavior or trait is effective in bringing about the desired result, then the brain's *sensorimotor cortex* and *infralimbic cortex* work together to strengthen the neural connections and help transform the new actions into habits so we can sustain them for the long haul.

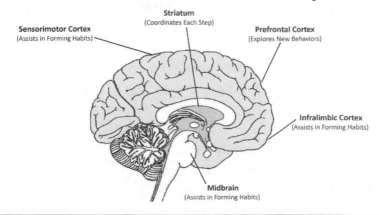

Striatum
(Coordinates Each Step)

Sensorimotor Cortex
(Assists in Forming Habits)

Prefrontal Cortex
(Explores New Behaviors)

Infralimbic Cortex
(Assists in Forming Habits)

Midbrain
(Assists in Forming Habits)

## TAKING ACTION

After someone has defined the new behavior they desire and planned how they will achieve it, they enter the acting phase of change. Hopefully, they have prepared themselves to meet reasonable goals along a manageable timeline. However, success may require a willingness to adjust that timeline if necessary. My friend Jackson began taking one flight of stairs up to his office the first week. During the second week of his program, Jackson graduated to two flights each day, but the third week he caught a cold and was too tired to take the stairs, so he had a temporary setback. Once he recovered, he was able to get back to two flights each day without much effort and was encouraged by the endurance he had built up in a relatively short period of time.

Personality change is challenging for many people, and it is not surprising that lapses and relapses sometimes occur. A lapse is a single slip back to an old behavior, while a relapse is a more significant backslide. Knowing that lapses are common during the acting phase and reframing them as temporary setbacks can help people avoid feeling out of control. If they allow themselves to bounce back to their new behaviors swiftly, they can avoid letting a minor lapse evolve into a relapse.

Some people find they can gain a greater sense of mastery over their new behavior when they intentionally plan a minilapse— perhaps a day off from their exercise routine or a cheat meal from their diet. They learn that they can return to their new behaviors quickly following a slip and gain confidence that they will be able to bounce back from any future unplanned setbacks. Therapists, supportive friends, wellness coaches, and others can serve as informal cheerleaders to help people stay the course during the acting phase.

Shirley's behavior therapist taught her ways to better manage her anxiety and its accompanying symptoms. She started using a guided meditation app on her smartphone that she began using every morning as well as throughout the day when she needed to calm her worries. One morning she couldn't find her wallet and was late for work, and it threw her into a panic. For the next few days, her meditation app didn't seem to help. Luckily she had the good sense to call her therapist, who was able to reassure her that her lapse was temporary and she could recover quickly. That brief phone call was enough to get her back on track and make her feel greater control over her anxiety once again.

## SUSTAINING

Once our new, improved behaviors and thinking patterns transition into new habits, we move into the sustaining phase. Most of us feel a sense of relief when we make it to this phase, and many begin aiming for new and perhaps loftier goals—this time with the confidence that comes with having achieved their original objectives. Keep in mind, however, that lapses can still occur, so we need to learn strategies for minimizing and rebounding from a slip. Soon enough, our new habits will lead to permanent change and the possibility of a lapse diminishes.

Reminding ourselves of the values and motivations that first led us to change will help us stay the course and avoid setbacks. Remaining close to others who share our ideals and support our new desired behaviors is important for a successful and sustained personality change.

Jackson made it to the sustaining phase—he was able to lose 30 pounds with his diet and exercise program, but he wanted to do more. After six months on his program, he finally agreed to join me at the gym and meet my trainer. Jackson began strength training on the weekends, and with the trainer's encouragement, he increased his cardiovascular workouts as well. Jackson understood that his new diet and active lifestyle would protect his health over the years, and although he no longer was a go-to choice to play Santa Claus, he remained his jolly old self.

## CHANGE STRATEGIES THAT WORK

No matter what phase you have reached in your quest for change, you will discover that some strategies are more effective for you than others. By experimenting with different approaches, you will find the ones that work best for you. If you encounter an unforeseen snag with one approach, you may wish to abandon it for a different method. Mental flexibility is key for discovering what motivates you and overcoming the barriers that may be holding you back.

One principle that drives many of our decisions about behavior change is known as *operant conditioning*. This is a form of learning that occurs when a consequence of a behavior reinforces that behavior. For example, we know that Emma from chapter 1 is a naturally shy individual, and her reclusiveness leads to feelings of loneliness. If she were to become more outgoing, she could create new friendships that would mitigate her sense of isolation. The pleasurable feelings she would experience when she gets out and spends time with new people would be the positive consequence that reinforces her new, outgoing behavior. Of course, a barrier to achieving the popularity she desires may be the initial anxiety she experiences while trying to be more extroverted. If she were to focus on ways to cope better with her anxiety, Emma would have a better chance of minimizing it and overcoming the barrier it poses to her changing.

# EFFECTIVE STRATEGIES FOR CHANGE

- *Detail your reasons for changing.* Knowing the benefits of new behaviors will keep you motivated. Gathering information and talking with experts can provide a strong rationale and will help you stick with your new behaviors. The more clearly you detail and define your goals, the smoother you will move through the phases and achieve them.

- *Identify your barriers.* Whether it's old bad habits, current unhealthy relationships, or any other forces holding you back, making an inventory of your barriers to change will help you identify and overcome them.

- *Process your feelings.* Anxiety, guilt, and other uncomfortable emotions often reinforce old behaviors and create barriers to change unless they are thought through and understood. Self-reflection, candid chats with people you trust, or psychotherapy can be effective in elucidating such emotions.

- *Strengthen your support system.* The scientific evidence is compelling that strong social support is key to successful behavior change. Spending time with like-minded individuals who share your goals and who can cheer you on will increase your likelihood of success.

- *Shoot for reasonable goals.* People often set the bar way too high for success. Achieving a series of smaller goals rather than trying to do everything at once is more likely to lead you to success.

- *Prepare for lapses.* Remind yourself that a lapse here or there is common. Anticipate and try not to embrace them as failures. Instead, reframe them as temporary setbacks so you can quickly regain a sense of control.

- *Readjust your approach when necessary.* Despite your best efforts, you may find that you keep lapsing back to your old ways. That's when it's time to step back, review your goals and motivations, and possibly try an alternative strategy.

As you read ahead, you will get a better idea of your base-line personality, future goals, and how to achieve them. Making a commitment to taking action, defining your end point, and sticking to your program is the formula that has helped many of my patients achieve their goals and become who they wish to be.

# CHAPTER 3

## Assess Yourself and Define Your Goals

*Who in the world am I? Ah, that's the great puzzle.*
—Lewis Carroll

THE SCIENTIFIC EVIDENCE INDICATES that our personalities have an impact on almost every aspect of our lives, including our physical health, mental well-being, social relationships, educational achievement, financial stability, and even life expectancy. Most of us seek personality change as a means to an end— we want to change one or more aspects of our personality in order to achieve a certain goal and improve our lives. Before you try to change your personality, it's essential to define the goals you wish to attain in your life.

### DEFINING GOALS

Self-awareness and honest introspection are vital to successful personality change, and when I help patients identify their goals, we usually begin with broad strokes. Once we have a general list of goals, we can start to fill in the details and set a course for achieving the desired changes.

Begin by answering the questions below:

- What kind of person do you want to become?

   _____

   _____

- How would you like other people to think of you?

   _____

   _____

- What would your ideal lifestyle look like?

   _____

   _____

- What do you feel passionate about?

   _____

   _____

- If a magic genie granted you one wish, what would it be?

   _____

   _____

Your answers above will help point you to your general goals, such as improved relationships, increased financial success, or a healthy lifestyle. To further hone in on the specifics of what you wish to achieve, consider these more defined goals that many people share:

- *Career.* Increased respect, more autonomy, fewer hours, greater leadership role.
- *Finances.* Higher income, more savings, less frivolous spending, better planning.
- *Mind health.* More joy, less fear, greater self-esteem, increased focus, less guilt, reduced anxiety, better anger management.

- *Personal growth.* More empathy, higher intellectual achievement, greater creativity, more perseverance, increased generosity and philanthropy, more artistic/musical/literary appreciation, increased spirituality, greater resilience.
- *Relationships.* More friends, greater intimacy, stronger family ties.
- *Physical health and wellness.* Less pain, more energy, greater strength and endurance, fewer medications, better health care.
- *Lifestyle habits.* Quit smoking, better sleep, less alcohol, improved time management, healthier diet, more exercise, less unnecessary risk taking.
- *Appearance.* Weight change, improved grooming, better physical shape.
- *Environment.* Less clutter, better air quality, quieter home, less driving.

Fill in the grid below by specifying what, if anything, you'd like to change or achieve in any of the following areas of your life.

| Area of Life | What You Would Like to Change or Achieve |
|---|---|
| Career | |
| Finances | |
| Mind health | |
| Personal growth | |
| Health and wellness | |
| Lifestyle habits | |
| Appearance | |
| Environment | |
| Relationships | |
| Other | |

Now that you have more clearly defined your goals, go back and number them in order of importance. Prioritizing your objectives allows you to avoid the daunting task of trying to tackle everything at once and helps delineate which specific feature or features of your personality you should focus on changing first.

For instance, if your number one goal is to become more popular and make new friends, you will next need to discover which personality traits are holding you back. Perhaps your shy temperament makes you too anxious to meet new people. Maybe you are overly conscientious and your instinct to be in control chases away potential friends. If your goal is greater success at work, perhaps your disorganized personality style is stalling your career. Or maybe you have trouble getting along with colleagues and you need to focus on becoming more agreeable. If you're a person who gets stressed out easily, your high-strung personality may be hindering your advancement. An honest assessment of your current personality is essential before initiating any successful changes.

## ASSESSING YOUR PERSONALITY

When Steven, a 41-year-old attorney, first came to see me, he told me he was having trouble sleeping and felt anxious all the time. He suspected his recent breakup with his fiancée was triggering it.

"I'd been working 60-hour weeks for months, saving money for the wedding, and then last Friday, she dumped me and moved out."

"Did she give you an explanation?" I asked.

"Just some BS about my job being more important to me than our relationship. She thinks I'm too detached and secretive with her."

"Do you feel any of that is true?"

"Just because I don't like to talk about my work, doesn't mean I'm keeping secrets. And I'm not detached, Dr. Small. I'm probably the most open and approachable person I know."

Sitting at the far end of the sofa with his legs crossed and his arms folded tightly in front of his chest, Steven was not displaying very "open and approachable" body language. He also made minimal eye contact with me, which could be his way of avoiding intimacy. I imagined that this type of behavior might come off as detached to his fiancée. And Steven's reluctance to talk about his job—which apparently took up most of his waking hours—could understandably be construed as being secretive.

As I tried to gently point out these observations to Steven, he became defensive and said he didn't come to see me just so I could take her side.

Psychiatrists and psychologists can get a pretty good sense of what a person is like through clinical interviews and standardized questionnaires. When mental health professionals evaluates a patient or client, they ask questions to discover how the person relates to others. They also observe how the individual responds during the clinical interview. That information provides the therapist with data that point to patterns of feelings, thinking, and behavior that help define personality traits, specifically in the Big Five categories—extraversion, openness, emotional stability, agreeableness, and conscientiousness. During the clinical interview, patients tell their stories through words and nonverbal cues. In Steven's case, he thought of himself as open and approachable, but his words and body language conveyed the opposite.

Although these face-to-face conversations during an assessment can be very informative, they still have limitations. Cultural differences may bias the interviewer's perception of the patient. Also, a single interview is merely a snapshot of that person at that precise moment in time—the patient may be having a particularly difficult day, so an otherwise agreeable individual may seem testy and belligerent.

Even the most enlightened interviewers may assess a client based on certain assumptions and biases that can distort what they observe. Jason Dana of the Yale School of Management described a young woman who believed she had arrived 20 minutes early to a job interview. After doing well in the interview, she was offered the job. Afterward one of the interviewers said he was impressed at her poise even though she had arrived 30 minutes late. Believing she had actually arrived early, her calmness during the interview was misinterpreted as poise and helped land her the job. Of course, that same calmness could have been misperceived as a flippant attitude, depending on the interviewer's own beliefs and perceptions.

Experts have sought to limit such uncertainties in personality assessments by developing standardized assessment questionnaires. These personality tests provide consistent measures of a person's emotional state, motivations, attitudes, and ways of interacting with others over time. The interviewer uses scales to identify the degree to which any particular personality trait is present in the individual. By using the same questions for each assessment, personality traits can be measured in a reliable way each time someone is assessed. These kinds of tools are also helpful in determining if and when personality traits actually change.

You probably have heard of the well-known personality assessment tool known as the Rorschach inkblot. With this and similar projective tests, the clinician asks the client to describe what they see while viewing ambiguous images. The client's descriptions reflect their projected thoughts and feelings.

Word association tests utilize a similar projective method. The client is given a list of words and is instructed to say the first thing that comes to mind for each word. Some of the presented words are emotionally neutral (e.g., tree, table), but others are intended to elicit an emotional reaction (e.g., mother, fight). These projective tests can bring out informative impulses and feelings about personality traits that the individual may not intentionally wish to share with the examiner.

Another instrument, the MMPI (Minnesota Multiphasic Personality Inventory), includes 550 items that the individual responds to as true, false, or uncertain. It is usually administered by a trained professional to help with clinical diagnosis and treatment planning.

More recent research on personality has employed an assessment tool that involves a standard list of 44 questions called the Big Five Inventory, which has been studied in large numbers of people of varying ages and ethnic backgrounds. The individual's responses provide a numerical estimate for each of the Big Five personality categories. Shortened versions of this scale have been developed along with other instruments that provide similar information.

## RATE YOUR CURRENT PERSONALITY

To help you get a better idea of where you fall in the Big Five categories, I have developed the following assessment tool based on the various available personality questionnaires. You can determine where your personality stands right now by circling the number below from 1 to 5 that most closely describes your traits in each of the Big Five categories. After circling the numbers, tally your score—ranging from 7 to 35—for each category and write your score in the space provided.

## Extraversion

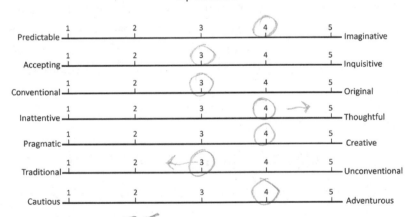

|  | 1 | 2 | 3 | 4 | 5 |  |
| --- | --- | --- | --- | --- | --- | --- |
| Quiet | | | ③ | | | Talkative |
| Laid-Back | | | | ④ | | Energetic |
| Thoughtful | | | ③ | | | Impulsive |
| Passive | | | | ④ | | Assertive |
| Reserved | | ② | | | | Uninhibited |
| Shy | | | | ④ | | Sociable |
| Indifferent | | | | ④ | | Passionate |

*Extraversion Score:* __24__

## Openness

|  | 1 | 2 | 3 | 4 | 5 |  |
| --- | --- | --- | --- | --- | --- | --- |
| Predictable | | | | ④ | | Imaginative |
| Accepting | | | ③ | | | Inquisitive |
| Conventional | | | ③ | | | Original |
| Inattentive | | | | ④ → | | Thoughtful |
| Pragmatic | | | | ④ | | Creative |
| Traditional | | | ← ③ | | | Unconventional |
| Cautious | | | | ④ | | Adventurous |

*Openness Score:* __25__

## Emotional Stability

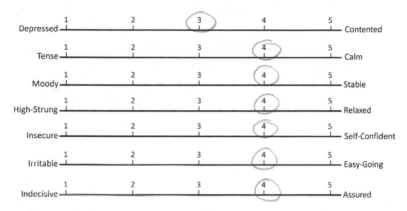

*Emotional Stability Score:* __27__

## Agreeableness

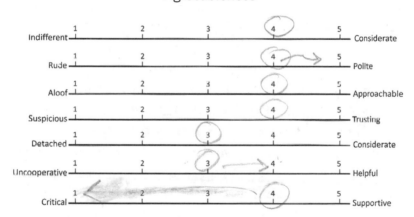

*Agreeableness Score:* __26__

## Conscientiousness

| | 1 | 2 | 3 | 4 | 5 | |
|---|---|---|---|---|---|---|
| Unproductive | | | | ④ | | Efficient |
| Scattered | | ② | | | | Organized |
| Messy | | | ③ | | | Neat |
| Unreliable | | | | ④ → | | Trustworthy |
| Resigned | | | | ④ → | | Determined |
| Inattentive | | | | ④ | | Focused |
| Careless | | | | ④ | | Deliberate |

*Conscientiousness Score:* __25__

Your total score in each of the Big Five categories provides information on where your personality traits currently stand in those measures. Scores in the 7 to 14 range in any one category are considered low; scores in the 15 to 27 range are thought of as moderate; and high scores fall in the 28 to 35 range.

Reviewing your initial baseline scores will help guide you toward which personality traits you may want to change in order to achieve your goals. Keep in mind that high or low scores may be good or bad depending on the context and your particular objectives. For example, a woman who desires greater career success but scores low on the conscientiousness scale may simply need to focus on improving her attention to detail in order to succeed. Another individual with a high conscientious rating combined with low emotional stability may also be seeking greater career success but may be suffering from an obsessive-compulsive disorder that cripples his ability to succeed on the job. That individual may wish to focus on reducing his conscientiousness score and increasing his emotional stability score in order to attain his goal.

## YOUR SELF-IMAGE AND HOW OTHERS SEE YOU

Sometimes our behavior sends a message to others that is different from what we feel or intend to convey. This can lead others to perceive our personality traits differently from our own self-assessments. You may be daydreaming about a pleasant day you spent at the beach last weekend, but your boyfriend might believe that you're being distant or perhaps feeling angry. Allowing yourself to gain insight into such discrepancies is an important step to self-awareness and realizing personality change. This process involves understanding how your behavior affects other people and how it reflects back on you through their reactions.

Many people judge themselves more harshly than others do. That disconnect between who we think we are and how others perceive us can sabotage our efforts to succeed and live a happy life. It can lead to conflicts in relationships, underperformance at work or school, frustration, and discontent. Sometimes our emotions cloud our perceptions of who we are. If you feel anxious, guilty, or depressed, those feelings can take center stage and make it hard to truly recognize how you come off to others. Even though these feelings are often transient, people tend to hang on to their distorted perceptions of themselves and others.

To gain further insight into your personality traits, you might consider asking someone you know and trust to also rate your personality in each of the Big Five categories and tally up their results. It's possible that your own perceptions of who you are differ somewhat from those of your friend. Although it can be uncomfortable if your partner or friend sees you differently from whom you think you are, an honest appraisal of how someone else perceives you can offer insights and strengthen your motivation to change.

# CHAPTER 4

## Extraversion 101

**Jerry:** *The walking date is a good date. You don't have to look right at the other person.*
**Elaine:** *It's the next best thing to being alone.*

*—Seinfeld*

"**HOW CAN I BE** of help?" I asked the young couple seated on my office sofa.

"We've been married three years, Dr. Small, and Jeff's already acting like an old man. He never wants to do anything or go anywhere."

"Come on, Lisa. We just went out with your friends Karen and . . . her husband."

"Mitch! His name is Mitch. And that was a month ago."

Both in their mid-30s, Lisa was a talent agent and Jeff was a physical therapist.

"I'm tired of sitting home and watching TV every night," Lisa continued. "It was different when we were dating. It's like his whole personality has changed."

"Do you feel you've changed, Jeff?" I asked.

"Well, no . . ."

Lisa raised her voice. "Of course you have." She turned to me. "He used to be fun. And he liked my friends."

"I don't mind your friends, or their husbands. Except for the boring ones."

"You don't make any effort to get to know them, Jeff. You just clam up."

"What is it like when you go out with Jeff's friends?" I asked.

Jeff started to answer, but Lisa interrupted, "He doesn't really have any friends anymore."

"That's not true."

"Friends that are couples, I mean."

I could see Jeff getting frustrated, but rather than correct Lisa, he just sat back and let her carry the show. The social dynamic in couples often tilts toward whoever's personality is the more extroverted, and Lisa's outgoing, perhaps even a bit overbearing personality clearly dominated Jeff's more docile style. I also noted that Jeff's passive-aggressive behavior toward Lisa might be contributing to her annoyance with him.

When someone is passive-aggressive, they express their angry feelings indirectly. Instead of candidly telling Lisa that he didn't want to go out with her friend's boring husband, Jeff went along and then expressed his anger passively by remaining silent and aloof.

As the discussion continued, I could tell they were both invested in the relationship and wanted to make it better, and I hoped they were willing to do the work it would take to get there. The tension between them was palpable, but if I could help them learn to listen and communicate with each other more effectively, they might be able to resolve their conflicts.

I suggested they try setting aside 10 minutes each day to practice a simple communication exercise at home. It is intended to help couples stop attacking each other during discussions and instead talk about their feelings and the behaviors that might be triggering those feelings. When couples are able to share their feelings with each other without criticizing or becoming defensive, it usually brings them closer together.

---

### SUPPORTIVE LISTENING EXERCISE FOR COUPLES

The first day, one person is the designated listener while the other is the speaker. Each subsequent day, the roles are reversed.

Sit facing each other and set the timer for 10 minutes. The listener's task is to maintain eye contact, avoid criticism, and make an effort to understand the feelings of the speaker. The speaker is instructed to stay on topic and also avoid criticizing their partner.

The speaker starts by telling the listener how they feel about something that is currently bothering them. The speaker should not criticize or become angry but instead simply express what is bothering them and how it makes them feel. For instance, instead of saying, "I hate it when you leave your stuff all over the house!" the speaker might say, "When you don't pick up your things and put them away, it makes me feel resentful and taken for granted. I always had to clean up after my brothers and sisters growing up, and nobody ever said thank you."

The listener's job is to remain calm and try to understand what the speaker is saying. The listener should not judge, correct, or take personally what they hear. They can ask the speaker to clarify any statements that are unclear, but it's often harder to be the listener than the speaker because the listener has to remain calm and keep their feelings to themselves.

After the 10 minutes, each partner briefly describes the feelings they experienced during the exercise. When practiced correctly, most couples end up feeling closer to each other and experience less tension in their relationship.

---

I had Lisa and Jeff try the listening exercise before the end of our session, and they definitely seemed less angry afterward. Before they left, we made an appointment for the following week, and I felt I had enough information to begin formulating how I might help them further.

For a therapist, treating couples is often more complex than treating an individual. The therapist must deal with the psychological perspectives and motivations of two people instead of one and often has to serve as a referee between them.

In this case, I knew that if I focused my probing and interpretations too much on Jeff, he may feel cornered and alone. However, if I shifted my support more to Jeff, Lisa might feel misunderstood and abandoned. It was important that I balance my supportive and interpretative comments as well as pay attention to my own reactions and feelings about the situation so as not let them bias me.

The next session Jeff arrived on his own, apologizing for Lisa who got hung up with a last-minute crisis at work. Jeff filled me in on how well the listening exercises were going for them and said that he was feeling more hopeful about the relationship than he had in a while.

I was struck by how different Jeff seemed this visit. He was engaging, confident, and certainly more outgoing than he was in our first meeting. In fact, in the absence of his wife, Jeff seemed to shine.

We discussed the issues in the marriage as he saw them. He said he loved Lisa very much, but when she acted pushy and bossy, his natural response was to retreat and get quiet. He didn't like to get into it with her because it always led to a fight.

"When you get quiet, how does she react?"

"I guess it just pisses her off more."

"When you feel angry, Jeff, what would you tell Lisa if you could say anything you wanted?"

"For one thing, I'd tell her that I'm sick of hanging out with her friends every weekend."

"Go on . . ." I urged.

"I want an equal say in what we do. And I hate it when she yells at me."

"How does it make you feel when she yells?"

"Like a little boy being scolded by his mother. My mom used to scream a lot when I was growing up."

## HOW EXTROVERTED ARE YOU?

Ask anyone whether they believe they are introverted or extroverted and they will probably identify quickly with one or the other extreme on this personality-trait spectrum. The reality is that even the most die-hard extrovert has some introverted traits, which vary depending on the situation. Most of us are *ambiverts*–a combination of extrovert and introvert. Before we can focus on change, it's important to get an objective estimate of where we stand on the extraversion/introversion continuum. Place a check next to each statement below that describes you:

☐    I am comfortable taking risks.

☐    I work well in groups.

☐    I enjoy making small talk.

☐    Status and wealth are important to me.

☐    I become energized when I'm around others.

☐    I prefer spending time with friends over being alone.

☐    I'm more of a doer than a thinker.

☐    I usually answer my phone before it goes to voicemail.

☐    I often have a hard time settling down and concentrating.

☐    I'd rather talk about my ideas than express them in writing.

     If you checked five or more statements, it is likely you are an extrovert. If you checked fewer statements, you are probably more of an introvert.

Jeff said it felt good to be able to express his feelings openly, and I encouraged him to try to share those feelings with Lisa—perhaps the next time they did their supportive listening exercise. He continued to be enthusiastic and animated throughout the rest of the session, and it was hard to believe he was the same quiet and reserved person I met the week before. I realized that both he and Lisa had extroverted personalities, but when they were together, Jeff became introverted and quiet, which in turn exasperated Lisa. One of my goals would be to help them adjust their outgoing traits to meet somewhere in the middle.

They both returned for the third session, and as I anticipated, Jeff acted more withdrawn and introverted like he had the first time we met. I asked them each to complete a brief questionnaire to rate their own personalities. Not surprisingly, they both scored high on the extraversion scale, although Lisa's score was higher.

## DO OPPOSITES ATTRACT?

Many of us are attracted to people who possess personality traits similar to our own. If you are an extrovert, you probably enjoy socializing and become invigorated through your relationships. You wouldn't necessarily want to marry an introvert who shies away from parties and prefers curling up with a good book. However, in some instances, opposites attract as well. People are often drawn to others whose personality traits balance out their own. If you're an extrovert who has the gift of gab, it can be comforting to spend time with someone more introverted who has a penchant for listening.

After several weeks of couples therapy, Jeff realized that Lisa's bubbly personality actually comforted him. It gave him a chance to kick back and take a break—a minivacation from always having to be "on" at work and outside the marriage.

Lisa's reaction to this insight was mixed—part of her enjoyed when Jeff allowed her to command the social stage, but she also resented it when Jeff didn't participate socially and made her put in all the effort. For their relationship to succeed, Lisa and Jeff had to find a middle ground where they could both express themselves and still feel supported and appreciated.

Psychologist Carl Jung described individual psychological differences such as extraversion and introversion as dichotomies, and he noted how each of us naturally responds to these variances in others. When an introvert and an extrovert get together, the extrovert usually takes center stage. When two extroverts come together, each one's desire to take the lead can sometimes result in competition and discord.

## UPS AND DOWNS OF EXTRAVERSION AND INTROVERSION

Extroverts are known to be action oriented: They love meeting new people and get a charge out of social events. They are talkative, friendly, and outgoing. It is easy for them to make friends, and they often develop large social networks. Some extroverts make a habit of striking up conversations with complete strangers, and many find that talking with people helps them organize their thoughts and ideas. Individuals with extroverted personalities tend to draw in others, and most of us find them approachable and likable. The person who walks up to you and introduces himself at a party is most likely an extrovert.

People who are extroverted enjoy many benefits. Their extensive social circle feeds their mental energy. Conversations inspire and refresh them, and the attention they receive brings out their best qualities. After a tough day at work, an extrovert will want to review the details with a spouse, friend, or family member, as opposed to an introvert, who would rather spend time alone reflecting on the issues of the day.

These outgoing social traits help extroverts excel in both their professional and social lives, and they are often natural leaders. Your team captain, principal, or boss is more likely an extrovert than an introvert.

An extroverted person's strong social ties also predict better health outcomes and lower stress levels. Their empathic friends can make them feel better when they tell them about their problems and they receive both practical and emotional support. Multiple studies have shown that those of us who have more satisfying relationships live longer and suffer from fewer medical illnesses. Social relationships even have an impact on physiological processes, lowering levels of stress hormones, improving mental and physical health, and increasing survival rates by 50 percent. By contrast, loners are at greater risk for depression, which increases illness risks and mortality rates.

## BIOLOGICAL DIFFERENCES BETWEEN EXTROVERTS AND INTROVERTS

Psychologist Hans Eysenck differentiated extroverts from introverts according to their levels of arousal. Extroverts crave stimulation to feel satisfied, whereas introverts need very little stimulation to feel content. The feel-good dopamine brain hormone triggers a more intense response in extroverts compared with introverts. When connecting with others, an extrovert's blood dopamine level spikes more than when an introvert socializes. Introverts are perfectly happy sitting home alone listening to music, whereas extroverts would probably prefer going out to a concert with a group of friends. We know that introverts can be more cerebral and thoughtful, and brain scans show that introverts have thicker frontal lobes, the brain region controlling problem solving and deep thinking.

It is not surprising that introverts are less impulsive than extroverts, who may act recklessly as they chase after the next dopamine rush. They also differ in their genetic makeup, particularly in the hereditary variants of the brain's reward system.

Each end of the extraversion/introversion spectrum provided our ancient ancestors with a survival advantage. Extraversion offered the evolutionary advantage of group living and protection from predators, while quieter introverts may have been more keenly aware of their environment from moment to moment, allowing them to notice and avoid impending dangers more quickly.

All our personality traits fall on a continuum, and depending on the situation or company we keep, our degree of extraversion will vary. When taken to the extreme, both extraversion and introversion can have negative impacts on a person's life. Rather than friendly and outgoing, extroverts sometimes come off as needy, attention seeking, and distractible. Spending time alone can leave them feeling isolated, listless, and uninspired. They tend to talk a lot and are not great listeners, which can impair their social intelligence. It's not surprising that some extroverts have many superficial friends but few if any close, trusted companions.

Extroverted leaders may feel the need to be the center of attention and thus miss important cues to the needs of others. Their desire to constantly be surrounded by people limits their downtime when they might delve deeper into problems that require creative solutions. Their tendency to act before they think can lead to bad decision making and unnecessary risk taking. Extroverts become very excited about potential rewards and often ignore looming dangers, and they have a greater risk for hospitalization due to injury than do introverts.

## THE INTROVERSION/EXTRAVERSION CONTINUUM

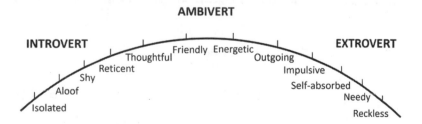

In today's society, we have a bias toward extraversion—our education system emphasizes group learning, and offices are designed in an open plan to foster collaboration. By many surveys, about one-third of the population is considered to be introverted, which is often equated with shyness and thoughtfulness. Although the attributes of shyness and thoughtfulness overlap, they definitely differ. People who are shy often experience social anxiety—they fear being judged by others, which influences their behavior. By contrast, many thoughtful introverts do like social situations, although they may prefer to remain quiet as opposed to engaging with the group.

Introverts are not always the most popular individuals, but their few close friendships may be particularly rewarding. Their thoughtfulness helps them make better choices when they act, and their quiet demeanor makes them good listeners, which exposes them to new ideas. The comfort with solitude introverts experience also provides opportunities to delve deeply into problems, which enhances their creativity and ability to solve problems. Introverts also tend to have much better mental focus than extroverts.

However, introversion has its downside too. Sometimes introverts get so wrapped up in themselves and their inner dialogues that they come off socially awkward, snobby, or rude. Speaking in front of groups can be terrifying for introverts, and they are more comfortable writing, emailing, and texting, which allow them to avoid the social anxiety they may experience during face-to-face communication. Their wish to blend in makes them harder to notice, and it is challenging for them to make new friends, date, and develop intimate relationships.

## POSITIVE AND NEGATIVE TRAITS OF
## EXTROVERTS AND INTROVERTS

| Extroverts | |
|---|---|
| *Positive* | *Negative* |
| Approachable | Attention seeking |
| Assertive | Distractible |
| Daring | Impulsive |
| Energetic | Inattentive |
| Friendly | Needy |
| Likable | Reckless |
| Outgoing | Self-centered |
| Talkative | Superficial |

| Introverts | |
|---|---|
| *Positive* | *Negative* |
| Attentive | Aloof |
| Creative | Awkward |
| Deep | Isolated |
| Focused | Reticent |
| Introspective | Rude |
| Modest | Self-centered |
| Self-sufficient | Shy |
| Trustworthy | Snobby |

## EXTRAVERSION TO THE EXTREME

Several years ago, Gigi and I used to socialize with her friend from college, Vanessa, and Vanessa's husband, Greg. Vanessa was exceptionally outgoing and loved being the center of attention. She and Greg often entertained other couples at their home, and during those get-togethers, Vanessa would regale everyone with detailed stories about her illustrious past. She'd describe her thrilling early years in Manhattan when she was a model, her exciting but short-lived singing career, opening her own bed-and-breakfast in Santa Barbara, and many other exploits.

Although Vanessa was at her best in the dinner-party setting, it was sometimes hard for anyone else to get a word in edgewise. During one of those parties, Vanessa invited Gigi and another girlfriend to join her on a trip to Santa Barbara, where she promised they'd have a wonderful time and she could show them her old haunts.

Once there, Vanessa continually attempted to corral the women into listening to stories about her past local escapades, but Gigi and the other women had heard them before and preferred to go off and do their own thing. As a result, Vanessa's extroverted behavior amped up, and she became more and more desperate for attention. The personality trait that had seemed like an asset to Vanessa and had drawn people to her began to turn people off and left Vanessa feeling isolated and alone. By the end of the trip, Gigi and the other friend couldn't wait to get home and away from Vanessa.

People with narcissistic personality disorders possess many of the negative traits of extroverts and often come off as needy, superficial, self-centered, and attention seeking. Narcissists have an exaggerated sense of their self-importance and require constant admiration from others. Like other extroverts, they thrive on stimulation from others, but they can also become preoccupied with fantasies about success, power, and brilliance. Their arrogant attitudes push people away and can lead to relationship difficulties, depression, drug or alcohol abuse, and suicidal behavior.

Extreme extraversion occurs in several kinds of mental disorders. Patients with bipolar disorder (also known as manic depressive disorder) can be very friendly and engaging, but they have problems regulating their moods. They experience periods of heightened elation, known as mania, interspersed with stretches of depression. When the condition is mild, their elevated mood states can make them more sociable and fun—the epitome of an extrovert. However, when the manic episode escalates, the patient's judgment lapses. They become more intrusive and delusional and often engage in risky, sometimes life-threatening behavior. These disruptive and sometimes dangerous symptoms can usually be treated with medication and psychotherapy.

---

### DID YOU KNOW?

- Extroverts enjoy the company of lots of people but may not enjoy spending time with only a few close individuals.

- Even though introverts are naturally good listeners, they still benefit from talking to others, particularly close friends.

---

Extreme introverts can also have their fair share of psychological challenges. People with social anxiety disorder suffer from tremendous fear of being judged by others while socializing or performing, and they are crippled by worry that they will embarrass themselves. They often experience intense fear of talking with strangers and are concerned that others will notice their anxiety. Many people with social anxiety disorder also suffer from an avoidant personality, a disorder characterized by low self-esteem, sensitivity to rejection, self-consciousness, shyness, and preoccupation with being rejected or criticized. These individuals often view themselves as being socially inept and have tremendous struggles with their relationships. Various forms of psychotherapy can reduce symptoms in people with these and other personality disorders.

## YOUR EXTRAVERSION QUOTIENT:
## STRATEGIES FOR DIALING IT UP OR DOWN

I worked with Jeff and Lisa in couples therapy for several months, and their relationship improved considerably. My goal was to help Jeff express his extroverted side when he was with Lisa and encourage Lisa to allow her more introverted traits to come out around Jeff.

I combined different therapeutic methods, including insight-oriented and cognitive behavioral techniques, and the couple supplemented our work with some self-help exercises at home. Lisa and Jeff responded well, and after four months, they decided to discontinue their therapy. Over the years, they sent me email updates on how they were doing, and after three years I received a family photo of Lisa and Jeff at the beach with their adorable toddler.

The most recent scientific evidence shows that many therapeutic and self-help strategies can change a person's level of extraversion. In fact, extraversion is one of the personality traits that changes the most with intervention. Both extroverts and introverts have been able to achieve their goals and live more fulfilling lives. Whether your extraversion/introversion level needs to be dialed up or down will depend on your particular objectives for change.

Many famous individuals at the forefront of discovery, politics, and the arts have been extroverts, but several have been introverts as well. Our personalities are complex, but most forms of intervention can accommodate change in several personality traits.

## FAMOUS EXTROVERTS AND INTROVERTS

| Extroverts | Introverts |
| --- | --- |
| Bill Clinton | Albert Einstein |
| Boris Yeltsin | Barack Obama |
| George W. Bush | Bill Gates |
| Margaret Thatcher | Larry Page |
| Muhammad Ali | Mark Zuckerberg |
| Steve Jobs | Rosa Parks |
| Winston Churchill | Steven Spielberg |

Many people want to be more extroverted so they can advance their careers. Perhaps they are too shy in group settings at work or school and need to become more assertive in order to excel. Others may have challenges in their relationships because they seek too much attention and come off as self-centered. These individuals may wish to tone down their level of extraversion to get along better with their peers, and they may also benefit by becoming more agreeable.

While doing insight-oriented work with Jeff and Lisa, Jeff was able to acknowledge that as a child, he learned to be introverted around his overbearing father in order to cope with his anxiety. This insight advanced Jeff's quest to change and become more extroverted around Lisa, which improved their relationship.

Other types of therapy are effective in altering extraversion levels. A study of group cognitive behavioral therapy (CBT) for social anxiety disorder showed that nine weeks of group CBT increased levels of extraversion and emotional stability. This particular form of group therapy includes education about anxiety and teaches participants breathing and relaxation strategies to help them better manage their anxiety symptoms. The therapy also teaches people to monitor and challenge their previously unsuccessful strategies for lowering their anxiety. In addition, participants learn practical approaches for developing social skills, engaging in conversations, and becoming more assertive.

As you learn more about how you can change your personality to improve your life, consider some of the following strategies for boosting your extraversion quotient:

- *Push yourself to socialize.* Introverts often have little motivation to meet other people, but making an effort to show up for social events will naturally increase your motivation.
- *Opt for enjoyable social activities.* Find like-minded groups by taking classes or joining clubs that focus on topics that interest you. It's easier to meet people who share your interests, and often these settings encourage people to break the ice and get to know each other.
- *Take baby steps.* You'll need to step out of your social comfort zone, but it's best to do it slowly. There's no need to introduce yourself to 20 people at a cocktail party—set a more modest goal of meeting one or two new people, and consider venturing out with a friend who can make you feel more comfortable and encourage you to meet others.
- *Practice talking to people.* Try to leverage your fine-tuned listening skills to improve your speaking skills. Pepper any silent moments in a conversation with relevant questions and comments to avoid awkward silences and keep the discussion moving.
- *Reframe your anxiety as energy.* If you experience anxiety during social interactions, try to think of that anxiety as a form of excited energy that can enhance your conversation and encourage you to be more interactive.

If you believe that your extroverted traits are too extreme and you wish to dial them down a bit, you might benefit from some of the following strategies:

- *Take some alone time.* Deliberately spending time alone allows you to process your experiences with others. It will give you a chance to become more introspective and recharge your mental energy. Explore some solitary activities that bring you pleasure and try them.

- *Prepare for social activities.* Planning for your social interactions may be counter to your tendency to just wing it, but it will help you make a better and more profound impact on others. Think ahead about whom you will be dealing with and consider their point of view before simply letting your natural charisma take over.

- *Zip it and observe.* Many extroverts have a tendency to interject and speak while others are talking. Try making a conscious effort to remain quiet while actively listening to and observing the speaker. When it is your turn to comment, those observations will reveal your focused listening skills and strengthen your social connections.

- *Prompt others to speak.* Rather than dominating the conversation, ask questions that encourage others to talk about themselves—most people like that. Practice asking follow-up questions rather than throwing in your two cents about your own experiences.

- *Avoid small talk.* As a natural extrovert, you may be an expert at superficial chitchat. Try to steer away from such conversations and delve deeper. Instead of offering your latest opinions on politics or global warming, ask others about what's going on in their lives.

# CHAPTER 5

---

# Becoming More
# Conscientious

---

*Laziness is nothing more than the habit of
resting before you get tired.*

—Jules Renard

**H**OLLY WAS EXCITED ABOUT graduating college. She had attended a small liberal arts school that emphasized creativity and independent thinking, where she had majored in creative writing and minored in theater. As always, Holly was able to use her charm and sharp wit to get by.

She wanted to start working right away, but other than "something in publishing," Holly didn't really have a clear idea of what she wanted to do with her degree or her life. Her father pulled some strings and got her an interview at a small publishing house that was looking to hire an editorial assistant. Holly sailed through the interview—charisma and confidence were always an asset—and she landed the gig.

Her first week went well—she liked the other assistants, and the editor she worked for, Claire, seemed nice. Holly definitely had a lot to learn about the book business, but she was confident that she'd excel in this job like she had in everything else. Claire gave Holly two manuscripts to read over the weekend, and Holly was eager to get started.

Holly spent that evening and the next day reading the first manuscript. It wasn't a very interesting story, and it seemed to take forever to read—probably because every time she received a text or Facebook message, she had to go back a page and reread it. But she finally finished and scribbled notes on a yellow pad. Holly got to the second manuscript on Sunday afternoon and stayed up until *3:00 a.m.* slogging through it. She similarly jotted notes on her pad.

Monday morning Holly tapped on Claire's open door, excited to show off all the work she'd done. She proudly set the two manuscripts with her handwritten notes on Claire's desk and waited for her to get off the phone. Claire told the person on the phone to hold on and looked up at Holly. "Did you need something?"

"No, um, just wanted to give you these manuscripts I finished."

"Good. Put them on the table. And grab those two new ones—I need the notes ASAP."

Holly didn't see Claire again until the editorial meeting the next day, where Claire took the opportunity to critique Holly's work in front of the whole staff. She held up the yellow pages on which Holly had written her notes. "Holly, do you have a computer on your desk?"

"Yes."

"Then why aren't these notes typed up? I don't have time to decipher your scribbling. Karen, please show Holly how to properly prepare notes on a submission."

Holly wasn't used to being scolded, especially in public, and she suddenly hated the job. The hours were long, and there was a lot more work than she could ever remember doing in school. Her desk soon piled up with partially read manuscripts, stacks of notes and messages, empty potato chip bags, and half-finished cups of coffee. And she found out that her boss, Claire, was uptight; she got annoyed if Holly showed up even a minute late, and she always seemed skeptical about Holly's excuses for not following up on tasks.

After three weeks on the job, Claire called Holly into her office and fired her.

"What?! Why?" Holly asked. Claire had a long list of complaints about Holly's poor job performance and lack of conscientiousness: she was disorganized and easily distracted. Besides showing little dedication, Holly routinely missed deadlines and showed up late to meetings.

Apparently Holly's progressive, liberal-arts education had not fully prepared her for the real working world. Although she was bright, personable, and outgoing, she lacked many of the personality traits necessary to succeed in a competitive job market, including punctuality, organization, diligence, and efficiency.

This was the first time that Holly had ever really messed up at anything, and after the initial shock, she didn't know where to turn except to her parents. They suggested that perhaps a job guidance counselor could help get her budding career on track.

Holly made an appointment with Mr. Lambert, a highly recommended job counselor. She hoped he could help her sift through the want ads and avoid getting stuck with another strict and rigid boss. But Mr. Lambert said she was not ready for any of that yet. He wanted Holly to fill out several questionnaires so he could get a better idea of her strengths and weaknesses.

At their second meeting, Mr. Lambert gave her feedback on the questionnaires. Holly had several strengths that could predict future job success, but she also had some weaknesses that were holding her back. He pointed out her poor follow-through on tasks, lack of attention to detail, and tendency to procrastinate. Holly felt herself tearing up but pulled it together and asked him what she could do about it.

Mr. Lambert suggested they work to improve her overall conscientiousness. He had helped many clients with similar challenges, and if she were motivated to do the work, he could help her change her ways.

Holly was skeptical, but her fear of another failure was enough motivation for her to take Mr. Lambert seriously. He taught her to create to-do lists, schedule tasks more realistically, practice methods for remaining focused, and avoid multitasking.

---

### TO-DO LIST FOR HOLLY'S NEXT JOB

- Reschedule appointments to avoid missing work.

- Check GPS app to determine the amount of time needed to get to work.

- Get familiar with recent books on publisher's list.

- Take notes at meetings and highlight action items.

- Remember, no texting and no Facebook on the job.

---

Mr. Lambert even helped Holly learn to meditate and become more mindful. He claimed that meditation could improve her ability to concentrate on one task at a time, which in turn would make her more efficient. Within a few weeks, the new conscientiousness skills Holly was practicing started to turn into new habits, and that's when Mr. Lambert said it was time to look for a job.

After half a dozen interviews, Holly landed another position at a smaller publishing firm, and she found that all her efforts to change had paid off. She felt better organized and more efficient, and she was able to keep up with her assignments and tasks. Two weeks in, her new boss praised Holly on her creativity and dedication. After six months, Holly was promoted to a junior editor position.

## THE UPSIDE OF CONSCIENTIOUSNESS

Becoming more conscientious really made a difference in Holly's professional life, and if Mr. Lambert had repeated a personality assessment after they worked together, her conscientiousness score would have risen dramatically. The timing was right for her to change: the shock of that first-time failure caught Holly off guard and inspired her to do something to avoid another painful experience like that. Holly was beyond the considering and planning phases of personality change. She was prepared to take action and do the work required to make a change in her life, and her actions paid off quickly.

Conscientiousness clearly has its advantages. People who are organized, punctual, thorough, and trustworthy have a much greater likelihood of success in life. Conscientious individuals are better able to find a job and hold on to it. They also earn higher salaries and are more satisfied with their jobs than those who are not conscientious. They get better grades in school, score higher on tests, and feel good about themselves when they perform well. Because conscientious people are more likely to follow rules, they are less likely to end up in trouble with the law.

Conscientiousness is also associated with resilience, the ability to recover quickly from setbacks. If a conscientious person trips up at one task, the chances are they will have a plan B and be ready to follow through on it. Not surprisingly, conscientious individuals have greater mental focus and are less distractible.

Conscientious people also enjoy better health. They are more likely to take their medicines and visit their doctors regularly. They tend to consume healthier foods, exercise regularly, and not smoke. Such traits at an early age often predict future health behaviors: a longitudinal study of nearly 2,000 research subjects ages 11 to 15 showed that high conscientiousness predicted a lower risk for drinking and smoking while in high school.

---

**DID YOU KNOW?**

• As people age, brain size declines, but higher levels of conscientiousness help prevent brain deterioration with advancing age.

• People who score high on conscientiousness are less likely to read a tabloid newspaper or shop at a secondhand thrift store.

---

Conscientiousness is also associated with better relationships. By their very nature, conscientious people tend to be responsive and faithful to their partners and know how to resolve conflicts. Higher levels of conscientiousness are associated with lower divorce rates.

Conscientiousness, along with other personality traits like openness and emotional stability, has been shown to predict successful aging. Individuals with these traits tend to have longer life expectancies and better quality of life as they age.

## CAN YOU BE TOO CONSCIENTIOUS?

Clearly, conscientiousness is a personality trait that helps people accomplish their goals. But sometimes too much of a positive trait can become a negative attribute. For instance, I need to pay close attention to detail when writing books and research papers. However, if I obsess or focus too much on each little comma or word, I could get hung up on page one and never finish the project.

Conscientiousness taken to the extreme can be seen in obsessive-compulsive disorder or OCD. People who suffer from OCD often go too far when it comes to details and rules. They are extreme perfectionists and get stressed out when they fall short of their ideals. Individuals with OCD try to control others and have a hard time delegating tasks. They are usually rigid and stubborn and not much fun to be around. Fortunately, only about 2 percent of the population go overboard on their conscientiousness and have full-blown OCD. For some of these individuals, it can be almost impossible to function normally in the world.

## PHYSICAL EXERCISE BOLSTERS SELF-CONTROL

Conscientious people are able to set goals and follow through on them, and a recent study suggests that engaging in routine physical exercise can boost a person's self-control and ability to delay gratification. Investigators at the University of Kansas enrolled sedentary and overweight volunteers embarking on an exercise program. To determine levels of self-control before and after the program, the research team used a standardized delay-discounting questionnaire that assessed the volunteer's ability to delay an immediate reward for a larger future one. The investigators found that the exercise program increased the volunteers' levels of self-control, and the more they exercised, the greater the impact on self-regulation. The volunteers were reassessed a month after completing the exercise regimen, and although their exercise levels had declined, they sustained their increased self-control. Other research indicates that routine exercise improves function in the frontal lobe or thinking brain, the region that regulates decision making and planning for the future.

I have treated several OCD patients over the years, and I know that even mild symptoms can disrupt their lives. Richard, a 48-year-old accountant, came for therapy after his wife of 20 years divorced him. His diagnosis was apparent just by observing his behavior whenever he settled into my office for his sessions. He typically sat in the same spot and brought a pack of hand wipes to clean off a section of the coffee table in front of him. He would then carefully arrange his wallet, cell phone, keys, and glasses on the sanitized area of the table. I noticed that Richard's hands were dry and chapped, and I suspected that he was also a compulsive hand washer.

He admitted to being a workaholic, but he thought his wife was OK with it because he made good money. When I asked about hand washing, Richard said that ever since his wife left, he had become more concerned about germs and dirt. He added that his father had been the same way.

Patients with obsessive-compulsive disorder often have a family history of overly conscientious personality traits or actual OCD. Early life experiences can also trigger symptoms. People who have experienced physical or sexual abuse or other forms of trauma in childhood have a greater risk for OCD. In Richard's case, I learned that although he was able to get along fairly well at work, under stress his symptoms would intensify. Richard's anxiety over his divorce had escalated his conscientious traits into full-blown OCD.

Even though obsessive-compulsive disorder can cause tremendous disruption in victims' lives, effective treatments are available, including medication. Selective serotonin reuptake inhibitors such as Prozac (fluoxetine) or Zoloft (sertraline) are examples of antidepressants that have been shown to be effective in reducing symptoms. People with OCD need to be patient when taking these medicines because it can take up to several months for the effects to take hold. Psychotherapy can be quite effective for the disorder as well. Cognitive behavioral therapy and other strategies often help patients learn to change their thinking and behavior patterns so they can live normal lives. Richard responded well to a combination of medication and talk therapy.

Many of us can become a little bit obsessive and compulsive when we are under stress, and in some cases it can actually be a good thing because it may motivate us to get ahead in life. If your mild OCD-like behavior gets you to pay more attention to detail and make fewer mistakes, you will likely be more efficient and organized.

Like other personality traits, each person's degree of conscientiousness can be charted along a spectrum. Some individuals, like my patient Richard, need to tone down their conscientiousness level in order to succeed in life. Others, like Holly, need to work on becoming more conscientious in order to achieve their goals.

To get a better understanding of your own personality and level of conscientiousness, consider which descriptors in the figure below match your current personality. Many people have a combination of both conscientious and careless traits, although some tend to land on one or the other end of the spectrum.

## CONSCIENTIOUSNESS CONTINUUM

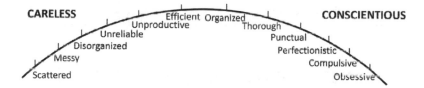

You may find that you possess some positive aspects of conscientiousness such as punctuality, organization, reliability, attentiveness, and efficiency—all assets for success. However, your perfectionism, obsessiveness, and compulsiveness may disrupt your personal and professional life if not kept in check.

## HOW CONSCIENTIOUS ARE YOU?

To further estimate your level of conscientiousness, check off each of the following statements that describe you:

___  I usually do a thorough job.

___  I am seldom careless.

___  Most people think I am a reliable worker.

___  I'm a fairly organized person.

___  I am rarely lazy.

___  When I take on a task, I stick with it.

___  I get things done very efficiently.

___  If I make plans, I follow through with them.

___  I rarely get distracted.

___  I'm generally a neat and orderly person.

If you checked five or more statements, it is likely you are a conscientious person. If you checked fewer statements, you probably fall more on the careless end of the continuum.

## STRATEGIES FOR BECOMING MORE CONSCIENTIOUS

The good news is that most people can become more conscientious if they set their minds to it. Consider the following strategies to help you become more effective, organized, and thorough so you can achieve your goals.

- *Assess yourself.* After reviewing your responses to the box above, hone in on which of your attitudes and behaviors could benefit from change. Do you have good mental focus or do you get easily distracted? Are you a planner or a procrastinator? Are you neat or sloppy? Do you work through tasks diligently or do you prefer dabbling in several things at once? Getting a better sense of your strengths and weaknesses in this personality domain will help you focus on the specific skills you need to develop.

- *Set priorities.* Conscientious people allot enough time for priority tasks and complete them by their deadlines. Instead of switching from job to job haphazardly, try listing your tasks and prioritizing them. Complete the most pressing task first, then work your way down the list.

- *Plan ahead.* Anticipating the future and planning ahead will boost your efficiency and organization. You can make this a regular routine by simply reviewing tomorrow's schedule before bed and preparing what you will need for each appointment the next day.

---

### DID YOU KNOW?

- Conscientious people are generally more politically conservative.
- Average levels of conscientiousness vary by state: people living in Kansas, Nebraska, Oklahoma, and Missouri are more conscientious than those living in Rhode Island, Hawaii, Maine, and Alaska.

---

- *Create to-do lists.* I began using to-do lists during my medical training because I had too many tasks for too many patients to remember everything on my own. Also, I was concerned that if I missed something, it could have a life or death consequence. I've stuck with the practice over the years, although now my action items tend to be more mundane (e.g., pick up yogurt and strawberries at the market). Many people use their smartphones to keep track of their to-do lists, while others use old-school yellow pads or clipboards.

- *Avoid multitasking.* When people multitask, they have the perception that they are getting more done, but in reality multitaskers are less efficient because they make more errors. Rather than jumping between tasks, try concentrating on one item at a time and complete it before moving your focus to the next chore.

- *Meditate.* Learning to be mindful and practicing meditation improves mental focus and attentiveness. Meditation has been shown to augment standard attention deficit hyperactivity disorder (ADHD) treatments and increase a person's ability to stay on task. It helps suppress distractions and random thoughts unrelated to the work at hand.

- *Mind the clock.* Review your schedule and try to allocate specific amounts of time for each must-do item on your to-do list. If you know that you have a block of time available in the afternoon for a high-priority task, you won't feel as much pressure to complete it in the morning when you have other duties to attend to. By assigning reasonable time periods for tasks, you can avoid mental fatigue and focus more attention on each one. Keep in mind that when you're busy concentrating on something, it's easy to forget about time and continue working on a task too long. Some people use the alarm feature on their smartphone to remind them when it's time to switch gears.

- *Get enough sleep.* One of the greatest contributors to disorganization is inadequate sleep. Sleeping less than six hours each night is a major predictor of on-the-job burnout. You might consider taking short daytime naps. Researchers found that when air traffic controllers took daytime naps averaging 20 minutes each, their mental focus and reaction times improved significantly. Keep in mind that napping too long in the daytime can make you feel groggy when you awaken and may be counterproductive.

- *Reduce clutter.* A cluttered, disorganized home or office can lead to anxiety. Clutter not only distracts us; it makes us less efficient. An MRI study performed at the Princeton University Neuroscience Institute showed that people who work in cluttered environments are less focused, more irritable, and less able to process new information. When clutter gets out of control, it can reach pathological levels and contribute to obsessive-compulsive disorder. About one in four people with OCD are also hoarders who suffer from a sometimes debilitating fear of throwing things away. Most of us would prefer to live in uncluttered, organized, and serene surroundings, but not everyone has the diligence it takes to maintain it.

    Setting aside time to organize and reduce clutter will increase your general efficiency. Many people find it helpful to schedule a regular time each day or week to file or throw away unnecessary documents, magazines, and other items that create clutter.

- *Create a routine.* Thanks to new technology, many people find themselves emailing, tweeting, and texting around the clock, never giving their brains a chance to rest. If you're trying to improve your conscientiousness, create a daily routine that balances both work and leisure time. If you feel mentally exhausted, it's likely you won't get much done until you've had a chance to rest your mind. Many people find it helpful to tackle their more creatively challenging tasks in the morning after a good night's sleep. When our brains are rested, they are better able to solve problems with renewed mental energy.

- *Get physical.* Recent research indicates that a regular exercise regimen leads to greater self-control and the ability to delay gratification. Even though the physical

# SIX TIPS TO TACKLING CLUTTER

To live an uncluttered and organized life, neatness counts. Here are six tips to help you reduce clutter and improve your life.

1. *Tackle one space at a time.* Attempting to reorganize everything at once will be overwhelming. Aim to declutter one room, closet, or drawer at a time.

2. *Create categories of stuff.* Get three boxes and label them *keep, toss,* and *uncertain.* Sort through your clutter and place each item in the appropriate box. Immediately discard the *toss* items, neatly put away the *keep* ones, and review the *uncertain* box again to see what else you can let go of.

3. *Get charitable.* If you believe your *toss* box contains items that might be used again by someone, call your favorite charity for a pickup. Discard the rest.

4. *Develop a sorting habit.* Whenever you bring anything into the house like mail, groceries, or clothing, try to sort them and put them away directly. It's a good idea to organize and store similar items together so they will be easy to find later.

5. *Stash rarely used items.* Seasonal gear like ski clothes and pool toys don't require a prominent position in the front closet during off-season months. Rarely used items should be stored in less-frequented places like spare bedroom closets or attics.

6. *Schedule regular declutter times.* Clutter tends to build up over time, so make decluttering a daily, weekly, or monthly habit.

exertion required for exercise is not always enjoyable in the moment, the discipline required to maintain an exercise routine teaches us self-control and reinforces the principle that present pain can yield a future gain.

- *Slow down.* Trying to get everything done at breakneck speed may make you think you're being efficient, but that rapid pace of mental activity will increase your rate of errors, reduce your productivity, and create stress and anxiety. Simply slowing yourself down can improve your accuracy, efficiency, and mood.

- *Eliminate distractions.* You may be completely engrossed in reading an important article, but if a blaring television or stereo in the next room continually distracts you, it will be difficult to focus your attention. Telephones, computers, and handheld devices are best kept on silent or out of earshot when you are trying to focus on a task. If you're working on a document, try silencing your email and text alerts so incoming messages don't intermittently distract you.

- *Consider a professional consultation.* If paying attention and staying on task is a challenge for you despite some of these strategies, you may wish to speak with your doctor to find out if a medical condition like ADHD is holding you back. If your excessive conscientiousness is due to obsessive-compulsive disorder, it can be hard for you to get anything done efficiently. Both of these conditions have effective medical treatments that can improve symptoms dramatically and help you achieve your goals. If you lack conscientiousness and your attempts to improve on your own have not helped much, you may want to consider psychotherapy. Sometimes unresolved psychological issues interfere with a person's ability to move on in life and become more organized and successful. A behavior therapist or wellness coach may also help motivate people who have trouble getting the job done by themselves.

# CHAPTER 6

## Learning to Agree

*My idea of an agreeable person is a person who agrees with me.*

—Benjamin Disraeli

**G**IGI AND I USED to socialize with Michael and Pamela, a forty-something couple we met at a charity event for our daughter's school. Pamela was sweet, and Michael was a hoot—a smart, successful, and opinionated financial advisor who loved kidding around and giving people a hard time. No matter what the subject, if I expressed one view, Michael would surely take the contrary stand.

At first, Michael's banter was entertaining and often generated lively dinner conversations. But as time passed, he grew more narrow-minded and intolerant of anyone who disagreed with him. Soon his rigid attitude and open expressions of anger became the norm, and we eventually stopped hanging out with them.

I remember wondering how Michael's investment clients could put up with his orneriness, and in fact his business had begun to falter. Michael's "my way or the highway" attitude and intermittent hostility turned off clients and left him feeling frustrated and angry most of the time.

About a year ago, Michael called me out of the blue seeking a referral for a psychotherapist. He said he realized what a jerk he was being and not only wanted to change but also felt ready to do whatever it took—his marriage depended on it.

I gave him the name of an experienced psychotherapist, but I was a little skeptical about Michael's motivation to change. It sounded like Pamela was threatening to leave him if he didn't make an attitude adjustment. My concern was that he might only be seeking therapy to mollify his wife and not actually be ready to do the work it takes to change.

I ran into Michael about six months later, and we had time to grab a cup of coffee. After a few minutes of chitchat about our kids and sports, I asked, "How are things going with you and Pamela?"

"I swear, Gary, that therapist you sent me to saved my marriage."

"That's great, Michael. What do you think made the difference?"

"For one thing, he helped me see that my habit of needling people for fun was actually annoying and off-putting."

He said he realized that the way he used to force his opinions on people came off as hostile, and he never meant to act like a bully. He was learning more constructive ways to express his feelings, and ever since he stopped trying so hard to provoke everyone, people seemed nicer and friendlier. Not only was his marriage back on track, but his business had picked up too.

I was impressed by the way Michael had changed his personality. He seemed more agreeable, relaxed, and easier to talk to. When he suggested we plan a dinner again with the wives, I said I'd look forward to it.

## AGREEABLENESS IS GOOD FOR YOUR MIND AND BODY

Agreeable people tend to be friendly, helpful, and trustworthy—that's why most of us enjoy being around them. By definition, agreeable individuals get along well with others—an asset in their professional and personal lives. They adapt to the needs of other people and find it easy to establish and maintain healthy and rewarding relationships.

Agreeable parents are easygoing and able to convey the warmth and nurturing support that make children feel safe. By contrast, disagreeable parents tend to overreact and get frustrated with their children, which escalate the kids' anxiety and insecurity.

If you are agreeable, you are resilient and adaptable, and although conscientiousness is a more consistent predictor of professional achievement, agreeableness has been shown to predict better performance in jobs requiring strong interpersonal relationships. Agreeable people are team players who help the entire organization succeed.

Being agreeable is also associated with better health outcomes, and people who score high on the agreeableness scale are less likely to be overweight or obese. It may be that disagreeable people have trouble stopping themselves from eating even after they feel satisfied, and this inability to control body weight poses negative health outcomes. Obesity increases a person's risk for cognitive impairment, heart disease, diabetes, and other chronic illnesses.

Agreeableness strengthens relationships, and stronger social ties are linked to better health and successful longevity. Dr. Thomas Glass and colleagues at Harvard University evaluated approximately 3,000 older adults to determine how social engagement influenced life expectancy. They found that people who spent more time socializing had a significant increase in their life expectancy compared with those who socialized very little or not at all.

Social support also boosts physical health. In a study of New York City traffic officers, investigators assessed blood pressure and other physical measures as the officers faced the daily stress of confronting traffic violators and issuing tickets. The researchers found that job stress spiked the officers' blood pressure, but when colleagues offered friendly support, their blood pressure remained stable.

The strong relationships enjoyed by agreeable people serve to reduce anxiety and lower the body's level of stress hormones, which can otherwise increase the risk for heart disease, diabetes, Alzheimer's disease, and other age-related conditions. The MacArthur Study of Successful Aging showed that people enjoying ongoing emotional support from others have significantly lower blood levels of cortisol and other stress hormones. Study volunteers who had stronger social ties required less pain medication after surgery, recovered more quickly, and followed their doctor's postop advice more closely.

---

### DID YOU KNOW?

- **Women consistently score higher on agreeableness measures than men.**

- **People with higher levels of agreeableness prefer Impressionistic art over Cubism and Renaissance art.**

- **Placebo or sham pain medicines have a stronger analgesic effect in people who are agreeable compared to those who are not.**

---

Other benefits of being agreeable include a stronger sense of personal well-being and happiness. Investigators at the University of Illinois and North Dakota State University found that this well-being advantage may reflect itself in personal choices.

Agreeable people are able to regulate their emotions, partly by putting themselves in happier situations. They usually opt for less time in negative scenarios and more time in positive ones.

These happier, more agreeable people are generally more optimistic, which lowers their risk for depression and increases their life expectancy. Agreeable optimists are also more likely to get timely medical help because they anticipate ways to improve or prevent their health problems. A positive outlook is also associated with a strong immune system, which protects a person's health by fighting off infections.

## THE DOWNSIDE OF TOO MUCH AGREEABLENESS

It is possible for someone to be overly agreeable. If a person continually avoids conflict of any kind, their agreeableness can become dysfunctional. Disagreements often need to be resolved rather than avoided lest they fester and lead to feelings of ill will. Left unresolved, these feelings may be expressed indirectly in passive-aggressive behaviors like pouting and procrastination, which can infuriate others.

---

### OVERLY AGREEABLE AND PASSIVE-AGGRESSIVE PEOPLE MAY SAY . . .

"I'm on my way."

"It was only a joke."

"I didn't realize you wanted it now."

"Everything has to be perfect for you."

"You look great for someone your age."

"Whatever."

---

Evelyn was someone who thrived on being agreeable, but sometimes she went overboard. She was excited about having her grandsons, ages 6, 8, and 11, stay for the weekend while her son and daughter-in-law went to Big Sur. A 64-year-old retired piano teacher, Evelyn loved doting on those kids, and they loved it too. Of course, at her age she would get tired running after the boys, but she adored doing things for her family and always said it gave her the most pleasure.

On Friday morning, before the kids came for the weekend, Evelyn's husband went off to the golf course while she spent the morning straightening the house. The kids were scheduled to arrive at noon, so she prepared a beautiful lunch. But they didn't arrive until 2:00, just as she was putting the lunch away.

"Grandma! Grandma! Grandma!" they yelled.

She hugged and kissed them and told them to go eat their lunch. Her son waved her off. "Don't worry about it, Mom, we stopped on the way."

Evelyn, disappointed and annoyed, held her tongue like always and asked, "Who wants to go swimming?"

By the time Grandpa got home from the club, all three boys were bathed, fed, and playing Monopoly in the den. Evelyn mixed her husband a drink and sat down to take a breather.

"What's for dinner, Ev?" he asked. "I'm starving."

The next morning Evelyn got up early, made waffles, and waited for everyone else to come down. When two of the boys announced that they hated waffles now, she made eggs and oatmeal for them. She refilled Grandpa's coffee and said, "How about we take them to the zoo today?"

"Oh, gosh, honey, I'm committed to a foursome at the club. You understand, right?"

Evelyn mustered a smile. "Sure, you go enjoy yourself. I'll take care of everything. That's my job." She meant it sarcastically, but he didn't seem to notice.

By Sunday afternoon, Evelyn was thoroughly exhausted and ready for her son and daughter-in-law to return from Big Sur and pick up the kids. They called to say they were caught in traffic and asked if it would be OK for the kids to stay for dinner.

Evelyn sighed. "Yes, of course."

When her son got there, the boys were already sleeping, so he and Grandpa carried them out to the car. Evelyn asked about the special granola her son had promised to buy her at the Big Sur Bakery.

He shrugged. "Sorry, Mom, I forgot."

Evelyn felt hot tears welling up in her eyes and a sudden rush of anger. "You what?"

"I forgot. It wasn't on purpose."

"God dammit!" she yelled. "I'm sick and tired of doing everything for everyone, and all I wanted was some goddamn granola!"

Evelyn, bawling, stormed up to her room and slammed the door, leaving her son and husband mystified.

Although Evelyn's lifelong agreeableness had generally served her well over the years, when she felt unappreciated and taken advantage of, she didn't know how to deal with it. She just kept doing and doing for others until either her angry feelings seeped out indirectly through passive-aggressive and sarcastic remarks or she blew her top. If Evelyn had had the tools to express her feelings in a more direct and constructive way, she might not have waited until she exploded in rage.

Even though agreeableness can be an asset in our personal and professional lives, sometimes the nice guy finishes last. Higher degrees of agreeableness are associated with lower earning potential. If you are timid and overly modest, you may not feel comfortable asking your boss for a higher salary. Also, being too agreeable can sometimes come off as insincere and groveling. The yes-man in an organization often seems disingenuous and would probably be the last person one would go to for honest advice.

---

**FOUR TIPS FOR CONSTRUCTIVE ANGER EXPRESSION**

A constructive expression of anger allows you to feel better about the other person and leads to less conflict in the future.

1. When you express yourself, try to focus on the issue that made you angry, not the person who made you angry.

2. Remain civil throughout the conversation.

3. If the discussion heats up too much, conflict resolution is unlikely. Take a break if things become too contentious and return later when you have cooled off.

4. Be sure to listen to the other person's side of the issue and acknowledge it when you are wrong.

---

Agreeableness or lack thereof has a greater impact on earning potential for men than for women, perhaps because being disagreeable is more accepted in men than women in our society. While a strong and decisive male boss may earn respect and obedience, the same behavior in a female boss may be interpreted as snarky and demanding. Also, agreeable people are more likely to be followers than leaders. The agreeableness personality trait is associated with a lower likelihood of becoming a manager, director, or chief executive.

The tendency to always agree with others is also correlated with greater gullibility and risk for becoming a scam victim. Overly trusting people are more likely to fall for the "once-in-a-lifetime opportunity" being offered over the phone or on the internet. According to the Federal Trade Commission, about one out of every five scam victims is 65 or older. As people age, they tend to become more laid back and agreeable, and con artists often take advantage of older adults with "grandparent scams," wherein they impersonate a needy grandchild and then dupe the senior into sending money.

## WHEN PEOPLE ARE DISAGREEABLE

People who are disagreeable tend to have quarrelsome personalities. However, sometimes these individuals act that way because they are insecure. They may be argumentative and obstinate to hide their inner feelings of being "less than." For such individuals, developing self-confidence would likely help them become more agreeable.

Our sense of self-esteem develops early in childhood. A chronically abusive parent or even one who makes an occasional negative comment at the wrong time or place can erode a child's confidence, whereas early successes or encouragement from parents can positively shape future self-perceptions. Our self-esteem affects all aspects of our lives, especially our ability to get along with others. Self-confidence makes us more resilient, upbeat, and better able to cope with adversity. Unfortunately, some people base much of their self-esteem on physical appearance and attainment of wealth rather than values, personality traits, and integrity.

Pessimism can also lead to disagreeableness. Having a positive attitude boosts self-confidence because we are more likely to believe in our abilities to solve problems and exert control in our lives. In the MacArthur Study of Successful Aging, investigators found that study volunteers who rated themselves high in self-confidence were more likely to believe that they could improve and maintain their mental skills. Self-confidence was also associated with better physical performance and sense of empowerment.

## POSITIVE AND NEGATIVE ATTRIBUTES
## OF AGREEABLE PERSONALITIES

| Positive | Negative |
| --- | --- |
| Considerate | Gullible |
| Cooperative | Ingenuous |
| Friendly | Passive-aggressive |
| Helpful | Pessimistic |
| Hopeful | Sycophantic |
| Supportive | Timid |
| Trustworthy | Undiscerning |

Researchers at Wake Forest University found that individuals who make a conscious effort to experience joy and happiness feel better about themselves and others. Study volunteers who *acted* happier by singing aloud, walking over and talking to someone, or being more assertive felt happier, and others perceived them that way. Making such conscious efforts to be outgoing boosts levels of not only agreeableness but extraversion as well.

Some forms of psychotherapy can help people overcome their habitual negativity. Cognitive behavioral therapy can guide clients on how to minimize their automatic negativity by learning to break the habit of responding to their negative assumptions and thoughts and learning to be more optimistic.

The ability to turn the other cheek and let go of angry feelings helps people feel more positive. Sometimes we hold on to anger toward someone long after we have forgotten the details of what the dispute was about. Learning to forgive others and ourselves will diminish such emotions. Dwelling on feelings of remorse or guilt for past errors rarely solves problems, and it certainly doesn't help make us agreeable. Research has shown that individuals who are inclined to forgive others are also more agreeable. They are less manipulative and more empathic and have a greater sense of moral responsibility. They are also more tolerant of rude or inconsiderate people.

## THE AGREEABLE BRAIN

Our brains have inborn mechanisms that contribute to agreeableness, feelings of joy, and a positive outlook. Dr. Richard Davidson and coworkers at the University of Wisconsin used functional MRI brain scans to pinpoint an area in the front part of the brain that controls positive feelings, optimism, and happiness. They studied one of the most powerful positive emotional experiences—a mother's feelings toward her newborn baby. The scientists found that when mothers observed photos of their babies, their brain activity increased dramatically in this frontal region compared to when the mothers viewed photos of unfamiliar infants.

Age-related brain changes may help explain why the agreeableness of older people can make them more susceptible to scammers. As people age, the area of the brain that detects deceit becomes less active. In younger people, this structure, known as the anterior insula, fires up when a person suspects a con artist, but not so much in a senior. UCLA neuroscientist Shelley Taylor and coworkers showed pictures of various faces to middle-aged and older adults (ages 55 to 84) and younger adults (ages 20 to 42). The faces were considered untrustworthy if they displayed averted eyes, smirking mouths, or similar expressions. They found that middle-aged and older volunteers were more likely to rate untrustworthy faces as trustworthy compared with younger volunteers. When the volunteers were asked to rate the faces during functional MRI scanning, neural activity in the anterior insula was minimal in the older subjects compared with the younger ones.

Other brain regions show activity when people make judgments about trustworthiness. Investigators at the Wellcome Department of Imaging Neuroscience in the United Kingdom found that in addition to the anterior insula, the amygdala, the emotional control center of the brain, becomes active when assessing whether or not to trust someone.

---

### GENETICS AND AGREEABLENESS

People can change their personality traits and become more agreeable using psychotherapy or self-help strategies; however, the genes we inherit can also affect our propensity to get along with others. Investigators at Yale University and the University of Connecticut studied people born with a copy of a variation of the alcohol dehydrogenase 4 gene called ADH4 and found it determined the volunteers' agreeableness trait to a certain degree. The ADH4 genetic variant is also associated with an increased risk of alcoholism. In other large-scale human genome studies, scientists have found additional genes that contribute to agreeableness and other personality traits. Studies of identical twins revealed that only about 40 percent of the average person's agreeableness trait is inherited—the rest is determined by nongenetic factors such as upbringing and environment.

---

The brain neurotransmitter serotonin, which is depleted in people with depression, is associated with higher levels of agreeableness. In experiments that reduced serotonin levels, research volunteers became more aggressive and impulsive. By contrast, drugs that enhance serotonin levels can decrease levels of aggression. Investigators at McGill University in Montreal, Canada, performed a double-blind, placebo-controlled study using tryptophan (an amino acid that induces restfulness and increases serotonin levels). They found that at a dose of three grams daily for two weeks, the tryptophan significantly reduced quarrelsome behavior and increased agreeableness in study volunteers.

People who are agreeable have more empathy, which is the ability to understand another person's emotional experience, and neuroscientists have pinpointed areas of the brain that control empathic skills. Dr. Tania Singer's research group at the Institute of Neurology at University College in London used MRI scans to measure brain activity in volunteers observing someone they love feeling pain such as a finger prick. Watching a loved one experience pain triggers the anterior insula, the same emotional brain center that gets activated when we feel pain ourselves.

---

## RATE YOUR LEVEL OF AGREEABLENESS

To get a better idea of your degree of agreeableness, place a check mark next to each statement that you believe describes your personality:

___ I rarely find fault in others.

___ I am unselfish and usually helpful.

___ People don't see me as quarrelsome.

___ I am naturally forgiving of others.

___ People describe me as trustworthy.

___ I am generally warm and friendly.

___ Most people think of me as considerate.

___ I am rarely rude in social situations.

___ I enjoy being cooperative.

___ I'd rather agree with people than contradict them.

If you found that five or more of the above statements are consistent with your personality, then your agreeableness score is fairly high.

## TIPS FOR BECOMING MORE AGREEABLE

If given a choice of spending time with a good-natured, under-standing, and supportive person or someone who is irritable, short-tempered, and antagonistic, the choice would be simple for most of us. It is clear that being agreeable, but not *overly* agreeable, is a goal for most people.

If your current level of agreeableness could use a boost, con-sider some of the following strategies to help you become more considerate and cooperative.

- *Do the right thing.* By matching our actions to our beliefs, we increase our self-esteem, confidence, and overall agree-ableness. As much as possible, make choices and behave in ways that fit with what you consider to be moral behavior. Even a little act of kindness to a stranger or a small charitable donation to a worthy cause will make you feel better about yourself while bolstering your agreeableness quotient.
- *Concede graciously.* Admitting to your mistakes shows character and garners respect from others. Accepting responsibility and being open to the opinions of others indicate that you are reasonable, approachable, and will-ing to solve problems.
- *Think positively.* Scientific evidence indicates that when we make a conscious effort to be more positive, it pays off. Simply having positive and grateful thoughts will increase your optimism and cheerfulness.
- *Don't be a yes-man.* If you are overly agreeable and say yes to everyone and everything, you may end up feel-ing resentful and angry. Think twice before agreeing to things, and if you must say no, try to be diplomatic about it. People who are thoughtful and discerning rather than all-accepting of everything are less likely to be taken advantage of or fall for scams.

- *Identify your negative feelings.* Sometimes you may feel disgruntled and gloomy for what seems like no particular reason. Try to take the time to figure out what's really eating at you and you may discover some unresolved feelings like anger or resentment that you were unaware of. If this happens, attempt to identify the source of your anger: Do you feel betrayed, violated, ignored, disrespected, judged, or unappreciated? Getting to the source of your negative feelings is the first step to moving beyond them.

- *Express yourself.* Optimal agreeableness involves the ability to disagree at times without insulting others or pushing them away. Unexpressed or unresolved anger and resentment can fester and may slip out passively. Learning to express anger without aggression will keep it in check and make you more agreeable. If your emotions seem too intense to control, try walking away until you have cooled off. When you are ready to constructively express feelings of anger or resentment, be assertive without being antagonistic. It can help to use "I" statements and highlight your own shortcomings rather than the other person's. Sometimes writing down how you feel and what you wish to say before confronting the other person can help you put the situation in perspective and dissipate some of your discomfort.

- *Disagree without making it personal.* People tend to become defensive when conflicts arise or they feel attacked. Try to keep these discussions from becoming personal by emphasizing the ideas and opinions involved, and avoid judging or blaming the other person.

- *Learn to forgive.* Letting go of grudges will reduce your stress, make you feel more positive, and boost your level of agreeableness. Learning to be more empathic with other people and understanding their point of view helps us release our resentments and feel closer to others.

- *Consider psychotherapy.* Talking therapies can help people become more confident and agreeable. If your self-
  help approaches are not as effective as you had hoped, try
  to find a therapist you feel comfortable with. Cognitive
  behavioral therapy, insight-oriented therapy, and other
  approaches can make a very positive difference for people
  who try them.

# CHAPTER 7

---

## Taming Your Neurosis

---

*I'm neurotic about not being neurotic.*

—Gwen Stefani

**"I** DESPISE PSYCHOBABBLE, DR. SMALL, AND I don't really believe in therapy."

"I understand. But since you're here, would you like to sit down?"

Barbara, a 39-year-old television producer and first-time patient, mulled over the seating options and finally chose the armchair across from me.

"What can I do for you, Barbara?"

"Look, I don't have time to sit around discussing my potty training or daddy issues with you, Dr. Small. I need help right now."

It sounded like Barbara may have had an unpleasant past experience with a therapist, and I was hoping that she would be able to talk with me about it.

"What seems to be the problem?"

"I haven't had a good night's sleep in weeks, and it's making me a nervous wreck. Even when I go to bed exhausted, I can't get comfortable, and I toss and turn for hours. I need some sleeping pills."

"We can talk about that."

I asked a few more questions about the nature of her insomnia because it can take various forms. Barbara had difficulty falling asleep at the beginning of the night, as opposed to having maintenance insomnia, which is the inability to stay asleep throughout the night. Trouble falling asleep often indicates an underlying problem with anxiety, whereas maintenance insomnia often suggests a depressive illness.

"Is anything worrying you?" I asked.

She sighed. "Always. I'm a world-class worrier, always have been."

"I think everybody worries a little, Barbara . . ."

"Right, sure. But I'm totally neurotic. Sometimes I get so worried about making the wrong decision that I can't do anything at all. I just feel paralyzed."

"Is there something in particular on your mind?"

"Not really. Things are going good. I've been offered a promotion at work."

"Congratulations."

"I don't know if I'm taking it."

"Oh, no?"

"I haven't decided." She shook her head. "See? I can't make up my mind about anything."

"When do you have to let them know?" I asked.

"I'm not even sure I want to stay in this business for the rest of my life."

"Are we really talking about the rest of your life, Barbara? Or one decision you're having trouble making at this particular point in your life?"

"Good point. But it's happening with everything. I can't even decide which route to take to work—the shorter, winding one or the longer, safer one."

I wondered if Barbara had always been torn between the safe choice and the riskier one, and I suspected there was something in her past that fueled her indecisiveness. I didn't want to push her to talk about it though because she seemed so dead set against discussing her past at this point.

"Is anything else challenging going on in your life?"

"No. Well. It's my birthday Saturday—I'm turning 40. Maybe that's freaking me out a little."

"Birthdays can trigger a lot of feelings. What does turning 40 mean to you?"

"Nothing, really. But just talking about it makes me anxious, OK?"

"A lot of people don't like their birthdays."

As we continued to talk, Barbara began to relax a little and eventually revealed how dissatisfied and conflicted she felt in several areas of her life—especially her career and her relationships. Many of her friends had already started their own families—something Barbara wanted for herself—but she was losing hope because she wasn't even dating anyone seriously.

As I listened to Barbara describe herself, I was struck by how neurotic she seemed. Besides being high strung, Barbara was tense, worried, and full of self-doubt. It was possible that she was suffering from an anxiety disorder, but her emotional instability could also indicate a highly neurotic personality trait.

Barbara's ostensible reason for seeking therapy was to get help with insomnia, but it soon became apparent that her upcoming 40th birthday and promotion offer were triggering an escalation of her chronic anxiety symptoms. She had her mind made up on what type of help she wanted—a pill to take away the insomnia—but as we continued to talk, a more complicated yet fragmented story emerged.

In terms of the four CPAS phases of change, Barbara was stuck in the considering phase. She was dissatisfied with certain aspects of her life but still ambivalent about whether or not to make a change. She was struggling with barriers and excuses for not moving forward on any front, and her neurotic behavior exacerbated her anxiety and its uncomfortable symptoms.

I thought if I could engage her in psychotherapy, Barbara might be able to set specific goals and become motivated to change. When that happened, she would be able to move on to the planning phase. If people become truly motivated, there is a critical moment when they shift from wishing they could change to actually doing something about it. That tipping point can be different for everyone, but once they reach it, the road to change becomes a real possibility.

When our time was about up, Barbara and I arranged another appointment, and she asked about the sleeping pills again. I recommended she try some melatonin and sleep-inducing guided meditation first, and we could revisit the question of medication next time.

## NEUROSIS IS NOT GOOD FOR YOUR HEALTH

People who lean toward feeling irritable, moody, angry, or self-conscious usually score low on the emotional stability scale. They tend to overthink things and have difficulty making decisions. When times get tough, it's usually hard for these individuals to roll with the punches. Any type of threat, frustration, or loss does not sit well with them, and their temperamental nature may make them feel like they're on an emotional roller coaster.

The bottom line is that highly neurotic or emotionally unstable people have trouble coping with everyday challenges. Their emotional reactivity often leads to ineffective conflict resolution and an inability to deal with everyday stress.

As with the other Big Five personality traits, everyone falls somewhere on a neuroticism/emotional stability continuum, such as the one below:

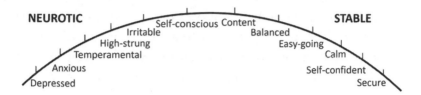

---

## HOW EMOTIONALLY STABLE ARE YOU?

To estimate your level of emotional stability, check off each of the following statements that describes you:

\_\_ I am pretty good at handling stress.

\_\_ I seldom feel tense.

\_\_ I rarely feel depressed or blue.

\_\_ Most people don't consider me a worrier.

\_\_ It takes a lot to upset me.

\_\_ It is relatively easy for me to make decisions.

\_\_ I am not a moody person.

\_\_ When a situation gets tense, I can usually remain calm.

\_\_ I rarely get nervous about things.

\_\_ I am seldom irritable with others.

If you checked five or more statements, it is likely you score high on emotional stability. The fewer statements you checked, the more likely you are to fall somewhere on the more neurotic end of the spectrum.

You may be familiar with some of the negative consequences of emotional instability. Neurotic feelings and behaviors are associated with a greater risk for mental and physical health problems, challenges at work, and marital difficulties. People who score low on an emotional stability scale are more likely to suffer from depression, anxiety, substance abuse, or eating disorders. Several studies have shown that neuroticism is associated with such illnesses as cardiovascular disease, atopic eczema, asthma, and irritable bowel syndrome. On average, neurotic individuals live shorter and less fulfilling lives.

One reason for their shorter life expectancy is that highly neurotic people often make unhealthy lifestyle choices. They are more apt to smoke cigarettes and have a greater likelihood of becoming dependent on alcohol or drugs, which partly explains their greater risk for cancer, lung disease, and cardiovascular illness. Low emotional stability scores are also linked to risky sexual behavior, emotional impulsiveness, and a lack of assertiveness.

High-strung people like my patient Barbara tend to continue overthinking things well into the evening hours and then have trouble sleeping. Neurotic individuals suffer more insomnia, which increases their risk for developing an anxiety or another mental disorder. Sleep problems associated with anxiety symptoms can also aggravate physical illnesses such as hypertension, diabetes, and obesity, which may further threaten brain health and increase the risk for cognitive and mood changes.

# MENTAL DISORDERS ASSOCIATED WITH NEUROTICISM

The irritability, moodiness, and indecisiveness of people who score low in emotional stability puts them at risk for a variety of mental disorders, including the following:

- *Anxiety disorders*
    - <u>Generalized anxiety disorder.</u> Chronic, exaggerated worry and tension that is unfounded or much more severe than the normal intermittent anxiety most people experience.
    - <u>Panic disorder.</u> Recurrent, sudden episodes of intense fear accompanied by physical symptoms (e.g., rapid heart rate, shortness of breath).
    - <u>Phobic disorder.</u> Extreme and irrational fear of simple things or social situations.

- *Mood disorders*
    - <u>Major depressive disorder.</u> Episodes of depressed mood and physical symptoms (e.g., insomnia, weight loss) that interfere with daily function.
    - <u>Bipolar disorder.</u> Alternating episodes of depression and mania (elevated mood).

- *Alcohol and drug disorders.* Inability to control alcohol or drug consumption.

- *Schizophrenia.* Chronic delusions, hallucinations, and other cognitive difficulties.

- *Eating disorders.* Anorexia nervosa, bulimia (secretive binge eating followed by self-induced vomiting).

- *Personality disorders*
    - <u>Antisocial personality.</u> Lifelong pattern of manipulating and exploiting others.
    - <u>Borderline personality.</u> Ongoing instability in mood, behavior, self-image, and functioning associated with impulsivity and unstable relationships.

## HEALTHY NEUROTICS

Despite these clear disadvantages to being neurotic, a *modest* degree of neurosis may actually confer some benefits. So-called *healthy neurotics* tend to be more conscientious—their manageable anxiety and mild neurotic traits motivate them to take action and get the job done. For those people who have neurotic *and* conscientious traits, their worries may be adaptive. Healthy neurotics still fret, but they are able to channel their concerns into constructive outcomes.

Dr. Nicholas Turiano and coworkers at the University of Rochester Medical Center in New York mined data on health, personality traits, and biomarkers of disease from a national survey of more than 1,000 participants from across the US. The investigators focused on an immune protein in the blood known as interleukin-6, which measures the degree of inflammation throughout the body. High levels of interleukin-6 indicate elevated inflammation that is associated with a variety of chronic illnesses. The research team found that the higher people scored in *both* conscientiousness and neuroticism, the lower their blood level of interleukin-6. Those individuals with low inflammation levels also had low body mass index scores (indicating less obesity) and fewer chronic health conditions.

People with greater neurotic and conscientious traits tend to be goal oriented and successful. Their worrying and indecisiveness can at times be troubling, but those traits also allow them to reflect on and weigh the consequences of their actions. Their conscientiousness tends to modulate their stress response, and healthy neurotics have the capacity to act in ways that resolve their conflicts.

Neuroticism has also been linked to creative genius. Of course, overthinking things can make even the most imaginative people miserable, but their ruminations can sometimes generate creative ideas that solve problems in innovative ways.

---

### FAMOUS NEUROTICS

Creativity and genius are often associated with a neurotic personality style. Here are a few well-known individuals who would probably score low on an emotional stability questionnaire:

- Woody Allen–his comedic persona stemmed from chronic anxiety and self-doubt

- Winston Churchill–struggled with bouts of dark moods when distressed

- Charles Darwin–often experienced an upset stomach and nausea when under stress

- Sir Isaac Newton–suffered from depression and at least one mental breakdown

---

## MULTIPLE PATHS TO EMOTIONAL STABILITY

Many factors contribute to an individual's level of emotional stability. About 50 percent of what determines a person's degree of neuroticism is inherited, which means the environment and other nongenetic factors determine the other 50 percent. Early childhood experiences, family dynamics, stress levels, and psychological support during development all have an impact. A childhood history of intrusive or distant parents, as well as physical or emotional abuse, has been shown to predict increased neuroticism in adulthood.

Several self-help and therapist-assisted interventions have been shown to reduce anxiety symptoms that are associated with high neuroticism scores. For example, cognitive behavioral therapy (CBT) is effective when delivered face-to-face with a therapist as well as when delivered through the internet using videoconferencing, texting, or messaging. The basic premise of CBT is that our thoughts determine our feelings and our behavior. Cognitive behavioral therapists help patients develop alternative ways of thinking and acting in order to reduce their psychological distress.

In one study of an eight-week treatment, participants with generalized anxiety disorder were randomized to either internet-delivered CBT or a wait-list control group. The intervention was a self-help program based on CBT principles and applied relaxation methods. The volunteers were shown how to use problem-solving methods to counteract their worries. At the end of the treatment, the subjects who received the therapy experienced significant improvement in symptoms of anxiety and depression, and those benefits continued up to three years later.

---

### NEUROTICISM AND YOUR BRAIN

Neuroscientists Michelle Servaas and associates in the Netherlands studied findings associated with neuroticism from multiple previous studies by pooling the information derived from brain scans performed on neurotic volunteers. The investigators looked at brain activation levels in these individuals while they were exposed to fearful stimuli or anticipated unpleasant situations. The research team found that volunteers with higher neuroticism scores displayed greater activity in regions of the brain's frontal lobe that control fear, learning, and emotional processing.

---

Worry exposure therapy, a form of CBT that counselors often use to treat people with phobias or irrational fears, can also reduce levels of neuroticism. It involves gradually and increasingly exposing patients to their feared experience, thereby desensitizing them to the anxiety associated with that experience.

Not surprisingly, many chronic worriers try to avoid the things that generate their worries. Worry exposure therapy is based on the idea that when people can identify and think through their imagined outcomes of their scariest concerns, their minds habituate to the experience, and the concern becomes less disturbing and stressful. One study showed that worry exposure was as effective as conventional relaxation techniques in lowering patients' symptoms of generalized anxiety disorder.

Psychodynamic or insight-oriented psychotherapy can help people achieve emotional stability through increased self-awareness and understanding of any unresolved conflicts stemming from past dysfunctional relationships. It allows patients to explore the psychological roots of their emotional distress, and its benefits continue long after therapy has ended. Although psychodynamic psychotherapy is usually performed face-to-face with a therapist, internet-based versions have been studied as well, and the research has shown that internet-based psychodynamic therapy can improve symptoms in patients with generalized anxiety disorders.

For my patient Barbara, the neurotic television producer, I focused on a psychodynamic therapy because I sensed that unresolved past conflicts were leading to her current distress. Although Barbara was reluctant to explore her past, I helped her feel comfortable enough during the first session so that she was able to return for a second appointment. However, when Barbara came back in, she looked drained and exhausted. She told me she'd been up since 3:00 a.m. after having a horrible dream.

"Do you remember what happened in the dream, Barbara?"

"Yeah, I guess. But I don't really want to talk about it."

In my experience, when patients mention a dream, they really *do* want to talk about it. I needed to guide her gently so she wouldn't shut down or bolt.

"Sometimes our dreams can offer clues to what's really bothering us. Humor me for a moment and tell me about the dream."

"Okay, fine. I had everything I ever wanted—I was VP of the network, I had photos of my kids and handsome husband all over my office, but I was still worried sick that I had forgotten or failed at something important."

"Then what happened?"

"It was bizarre, Dr. Small. I went into my boss's office, and instead of the network president behind the desk, it was my father sitting there, watching TV."

---

## INTERVENTIONS THAT CAN REDUCE NEUROTICISM

- *Cognitive behavioral therapy.* Goal-oriented, problem-solving psychotherapy that helps patients change thinking or behavior patterns in order to improve their emotional state.

- *Psychodynamic therapy.* Focuses on self-awareness and understanding of the influence of the past on present behavior in order to resolve conflicts and reduce symptoms stemming from past dysfunctional relationships.

- *Supportive psychotherapy.* Reinforces healthy and adaptive thought and behavior patterns to reduce stress and neurotic symptoms.

- *Worry exposure therapy.* Therapy that has patients imagine the worst possible outcome of their worries in order to dissipate fears and increase emotional stability.

- *Psychopharmacological treatment.* Antianxiety, antidepressant, and other medications that can improve emotional stability in neurotic patients with psychiatric disorders (e.g., generalized anxiety, major depression).

- *Mindfulness intervention.* Self-help or therapist-guided approaches that help people let go of worry and stress by focusing on their present-moment experience.

- *Relaxation training.* Any method or system that encourages relaxation and stress reduction. It may involve activities including meditation, breathing exercises, yoga, and Tai Chi.

---

"Go on . . ."

Barbara wiped away a tear. "He refused to talk to me or even look up. I felt like I was nine again—always in trouble and never knowing why."

I passed her the tissues, waited for her to compose herself, and asked, "What was your father like?"

"So critical, all the time. No matter what I did to please him, it was never enough. If I brought home an A on my report card, he'd ask why it wasn't an A-plus."

Apparently Barbara's relationship with her father growing up had left her feeling insecure and powerless, and these feelings lingered with her as an adult, shaping her personality. Barbara had always been an overachiever, but she was unable to get satisfaction from her accomplishments. She was plagued with self-doubt and was constantly second-guessing herself—even about what street to take to work. When I probed more about her anxiety over turning 40, she revealed that it meant her life was half over and she'd probably never be truly happy.

Barbara continued therapy with me, and we were able to unravel the ways in which her childhood feelings had shaped her insecure and neurotic personality. This relatively brief psychodynamic therapy led to real changes for her. She began to see how she played a role in distorting her current relationships by re-creating the dysfunctional relationship she had with her father as a child. These insights into her past gave her some perspective and defused those feelings. After just a few months, Barbara achieved much greater emotional stability. Her sleep improved, and it became easier for her to make decisions.

## NEUROTICISM VERSUS EMOTIONAL STABILITY: TYPICAL TRAITS

| Neuroticism | Emotional Stability |
| --- | --- |
| Anxious | Assured |
| Gloomy | Balanced |
| High strung | Calm |
| Insecure | Content |
| Irritable | Easygoing |
| Self-conscious | Secure |
| Temperamental | Self-confident |

## NEUROTICISM TO THE EXTREME

Time-limited, insight-oriented psychotherapy was effective for Barbara, but not all patients respond so well to this type of exploration into their past. For some people, delving into their childhood memories leads to intolerable anxiety that pushes them to the point that they lose touch with reality.

Early in my training as a psychiatrist, I was assigned a patient who was experiencing numerous neurotic symptoms. Edward was a 44-year-old man suffering from chronic self-doubts and difficulties in his marriage. He had been married five years and was convinced that his wife no longer loved him.

During our first few sessions, it became clear that Edward was constantly anxious and irritable, as well as overly sensitive. If he believed he was wronged by someone, he would fly into a rage, and it could take him days to get beyond those feelings.

My psychotherapy supervisor at the time focused his practice on psychodynamic psychotherapy, and he encouraged me to help Edward explore his childhood experiences, including his mother dying from cancer when he was 12. My supervisor thought that this early loss could have led to Edward's fear and anxiety about potential future losses like the end of his marriage.

As we continued to meet weekly, I encouraged Edward to talk about his earlier experiences, but his symptoms did not improve. In fact, they got worse. Edward developed insomnia and became even more suspicious and explosive. He was convinced that his wife was having an affair even though there was no real evidence of it. At times Edward felt so discouraged that he wondered if he might not be better off dead. He even started to get suspicious of me and questioned whether I really had his best interests in mind.

After two months of psychodynamic therapy, my understanding of Edward's diagnosis had changed. Rather than someone with neuroticism and generalized anxiety, he was showing features of a borderline personality disorder. Such patients are impulsive and have intense, uncontrollable emotional outbursts. Their relationships are chaotic, and they often suffer from depression and suicidal thinking. Instead of vacillating between normal and somewhat distorted or neurotic thinking, under stress these patients lose touch with reality and become psychotic.

Edward's suspiciousness escalated into delusions that people who cared about him were taking advantage of him. Borderline patients often have a disturbed sense of identity and are hypersensitive to real or imagined abandonment. His early childhood experiences may well have contributed to his sensitivity to loss, as my supervisor hypothesized, but he did not have the emotional strength and stability to face the anxiety that emerged when we delved into his past.

I shifted the therapy strategy from exploratory to supportive. Rather than continuing to delve into Edward's past, I attempted to bolster his strengths. During college, Edward had been an avid athlete who regularly went to the gym and jogged. I encouraged him to get back into an exercise routine, which seemed to stabilize his mood. Many studies have shown that cardiovascular conditioning can improve mood in people with mild to moderate degrees of depression. Exercise releases feel-good endorphins in the brain that immediately boost mood and reduce symptoms of depression.

Instead of interpreting his dreams and dwelling on his childhood relationships with his parents, I helped Edward cope with his current emotional distress in more practical ways through support, encouragement, and reassurance. I also prescribed a very low dose of an antipsychotic medication, Abilify, to help him regain a greater sense of reality. Within a few weeks, Edward's symptoms improved dramatically. He still experienced emotional ups and downs but no longer suspected his wife of cheating and had much less anxiety and depression.

A few weeks after we changed his therapeutic strategy, Edward came into the office holding a magazine and threw it on the coffee table. "Have you seen this, Dr. Small?"

On the cover was a headline about living with a borderline personality disorder. I surmised that Edward may have read the article and recognized his own personality described in a demeaning way. He seemed upset, and I wondered if he had stopped taking his medicine and become paranoid again. Perhaps he thought I was plotting against him and had collaborated in some way on this article.

"Did the article upset you, Edward?"

"Absolutely. At first. But then I felt sort of relieved."

I was pleasantly surprised by his answer.

Edward went on. "I recognized some of my own personality traits in the article, and it actually made me feel understood and less alone. I guess other people have the same problems."

For Edward, a supportive, structured, and practical therapeutic strategy was a much more effective approach. Reading an article that described his symptoms and struggles gave Edward a cognitive framework to better understand his issues. He clearly needed a more directive-based cognitive therapy, not insight-oriented psychodynamic treatment, which only stirred up his anxieties and made him feel worse.

I continued to see Edward for another year. After about six months, he no longer needed his medication. Although he continued to have some neurotic personality traits, he was better able to cope with stress and no longer presented borderline personality symptoms.

## STRATEGIES FOR ACHIEVING EMOTIONAL STABILITY

Even though neuroticism can be a crippling personality trait, the scientific evidence is compelling that a variety of strategies can reduce neurotic thinking and behavior and make life more enjoyable and fulfilling. Here are some tips to keep in mind to help you achieve greater emotional stability.

---

**DID YOU KNOW?**

- Women, on average, score lower than men on measures of emotional stability.

- People living in the eastern United States tend to be more neurotic than those living in many western states.

- Higher levels of worry in people with generalized anxiety disorder are associated with higher IQ scores, whereas higher levels of worry in healthy people are associated with lower IQ scores.

---

- *Determine your baseline.* Assess yourself to see where you lie on the emotional stability continuum. Do you tend to get depressed or moody? Do you handle stress well or are you easily upset? Would you describe yourself as a tense person or a worrier? If you answer yes to such questions, then you will likely benefit from interventions that help you become less neurotic.

- *Get perspective on your worries.* Stressing out over your worries doesn't help or change anything. Try to step back and consider what might actually be at the root of your concerns. Sometimes there are valid reasons to be worried, and when we are able to identify the root causes, we can focus on actions to resolve conflicts and reduce our worries.

- *Perform mindfulness interventions.* Mindful meditation teaches people to pay attention in the moment, which can reduce feelings of anxiety and depression and help maintain calmness in the face of stressful situations. Research has shown a clear link between greater levels of mindfulness and higher levels of emotional stability. Learning to focus on specific thoughts, feelings, body sensations, and the surrounding environment has a calming effect on most people. You can attend a few classes or get started on your own by downloading one of the many guided meditation apps (e.g., Insight Timer, Calm) available on your smartphone.

- *Practice other relaxation methods.* Deep breathing exercises, yoga, and Tai Chi are some of the many strategies that can help stabilize your emotions. You can learn them in classes or practice them on your own with the assistance of various websites and downloadable apps.

- *Get physical.* The scientific evidence shows that aerobic and other forms of exercise will improve mood through the release of feel-good endorphins. You don't have to become a triathlete to achieve the mind-health benefits of exercise, but getting into a daily routine will help make exercise a habit in your life and provide the best long-term results.

- *Go to class.* A classroom setting can be very good for learning yoga, meditation, exercise, and many other self-help strategies. People often find that answering to a teacher or coach is a more powerful motivator for change than simply doing it on their own.

- *Sleep well.* Getting enough sleep each night helps people remain calmer during the day thanks to improved mental focus and control. Because insomnia increases a person's risk for neuroticism, make sure that you get enough sleep each night. Self-help techniques like meditation, deep-breathing exercises, and progressive muscle relaxation can promote restful sleep as well as reduce symptoms of anxiety and insomnia. Talking therapies can be helpful, particularly cognitive behavior therapy for insomnia (CBTi), which teaches people to identify and alter the behaviors that disrupt their sleep. Several online CBTi programs are available (e.g., SHUTi, sleepio) so you can learn this technique on your own as well.

- *Transform indecisiveness into action.* If you're a healthy neurotic—someone with both high neuroticism and conscientiousness scores—you may be able to channel your worries into constructive outcomes. Rather than ruminate about the pros and cons of a particular decision, write them down in two columns and examine them objectively. This can help people get beyond their worries and distortions and reach a decision that relieves their anxieties.

- *Enlist a pro.* If your level of neuroticism is mild, you might begin with strategies that you can try on your own. Sometimes these methods have profound effects on reducing moodiness and emotional overreactivity. If your symptoms are severe, you may wish to begin with a professional consultation. Your internist or family doctor may be able to recommend a psychiatrist, psychologist, or other mental health professional. Depending on your particular symptoms, preferences, and baseline personality, a variety of therapies may help you change, including cognitive behavioral, psychodynamic, and supportive therapies. If you also have an anxiety or other mental disorder, psychopharmacological treatment incorporating an antianxiety, antidepressant, and/or other medication may improve your emotional stability.

# CHAPTER 8

## Opening Up to New Experiences

*The mind that opens to a new idea never returns to its original size.*

—Albert Einstein

**H**OWARD LOVED HIS MORNING routine. After jogging three miles with his best friend, Phil, Howard sipped his coffee, finished the *Boston Globe* crossword puzzle, and still had 40 minutes to shower and get to the office. He reflected on his four decades as an accountant and how well the job suited his personality—he was meticulous and quick with numbers, and many of his clients had become friends.

His game plan was to retire in four years after his 65th birthday. His wife, Audrey, was hoping they would have more time to travel and see the world, but she was skeptical that it would ever happen. Howard was not big on traveling; he didn't care for hotels or art museums, and shopping in tourist traps was not his thing.

Audrey sometimes got bored with Howard's predictable nature, but he was a kind and loving husband who provided well for the family. They enjoyed their time together even though they had different styles. Audrey adored new experiences, and Howard relished his routines. If they went to a restaurant, she almost never ordered the same meal twice, while Howard always ordered the same salad and entrée. Over the years Audrey had satisfied her wanderlust by taking trips with either her girl-friends or her daughter, Ilene, who had moved out west after college for a job in San Francisco.

That day Howard's boss asked to see him. The boss announced that the firm wanted Howard, with his many years of experience, to help open their new offices in Los Angeles. The boss trusted Howard to set the LA team up properly, and if he liked it out there, he could continue to work from the West-coast office. There would be a hefty raise and lots of other perks to go along with the new position.

When Howard told Audrey about it, she was thrilled. She loved the sunshine, and living in California had always been her dream. Howard was not so excited.

"Audrey, honey, I know you like Los Angeles, but what about those earthquakes and wildfires? Not to mention all the grid-locked freeways."

"Don't be silly, Howard. We'd be trading in these miserable winters and humid summers, and we'd be much closer to Ilene. It's like an hour's flight to the Bay Area."

"Sure, that would be nice, but what about Phil and our other friends? Who would I jog with every morning?"

"I'm sure you'd find another jogging buddy, and you could exercise outdoors all year round. You can Skype with Phil every day if you want to."

Howard had a week to decide, and he promised Audrey he'd give it serious consideration. Four days later, Phil dropped dead from a heart attack. Phil's years of regular exercise had probably extended his life into his 60s, but he had a strong family history of heart disease.

Howard was distraught with grief. It was the first time he had lost such a close friend. It started Howard thinking about his own mortality and how many more years he and Audrey had left. He began wondering why change scared him so much and why he was so set against the California opportunity.

On the way home from Phil's funeral, Howard turned to Audrey.

"Honey, I've decided. We're taking the job in Los Angeles. Life is short, and we've got to live it now."

She grabbed his hand. "I know this is the right decision, Howard. We'll make it work."

Six weeks later they relocated to their new condo in Los Angeles. The move distracted Howard from the loss of his friend, and although it was tough adjusting to so many changes, Audrey helped him realize that the hardest thing about the move was making the decision to do it.

Howard quickly learned the ropes out West and created a new routine. He figured out where to jog in the morning and the fastest driving route to work. He found himself enjoying Los Angeles much more than he had anticipated and even decided to delay his retirement—65 now seemed much too young to throw in the towel.

The short plane trips to San Francisco to visit Ilene made Howard feel more comfortable about traveling, and that spring they decided to take a family vacation together. Audrey was delighted—a whole week on the beach in Hawaii—and Howard didn't have to visit any museums.

---

## OPENNESS AND SENSATION SEEKING

People who are open to new experiences tend to seek novelty, and some of these traits are associated with very early-life experiences. People from Northern Europe who were born during winter months score higher on measures of sensation seeking than those who were born during the summer months.

If Howard and Audrey were given personality tests, their scores would be quite different on the openness scale. Audrey was very open—she relished new experiences and novel undertakings. Howard preferred his set routines and shied away from change of any type.

People like Howard who resist new experiences usually fear the unknown. They are comforted by familiar routines, and *new* often translates to *scary*. When Howard first contemplated the job opportunity, California didn't seem like an adventure of sunshine and fun. Instead it triggered his concerns about the unknown as well as his distortions about the risks of earthquakes, fires, and other disasters. However, a profound life event—the death of his best friend—prompted him to make a major life alteration. With the support of his wife, Howard grew more open to new circumstances.

---

### MAJOR LIFE EXPERIENCES CAN CHANGE PERSONALITY

Losing a loved one, surviving an accident, having a child, getting fired from a job–these and other major life experiences can lead to sudden and significant personality changes. For example, a recent study focused on how unemployment may influence personality traits. Nearly 7,000 volunteers were given a standard personality test twice over a four-year period. Approximately 450 of them were unemployed for up to four years during that time. The researchers found that the jobless men demonstrated continual levels of openness in their first year of unemployment, but with longer periods of unemployment, their openness diminished. The jobless women experienced sharp declines in openness during the second and third years of joblessness, but they bounced back during the fourth year.

---

## THE UPSIDE OF OPENNESS

People who are open to new experiences tend to be more adventurous. They love the opportunity to pursue different careers, hobbies, travels, or almost anything new and exciting. These imaginative and inquisitive individuals also relish novel and alternative ideas and viewpoints. Not surprisingly, their aesthetic traits and natural curiosity are associated with higher levels of intelligence as well as scientific inquisitiveness and discovery.

On average, people who pursue an artistic or scientific career score higher on openness personality assessments, and creative activity can be a form of brain exercise. For example, scientists have found that duration and intensity of musical training has a significant effect on brain anatomy. In one study of older adults, those who had received musical training during childhood, showed faster brain neural responses that appeared to protect their brains from age-related neural decline.

One aspect of intelligence associated with openness is known as *crystallized intelligence,* which involves the acquisition of new knowledge. Putting oneself into new situations offers opportunities to acquire novel information and expand our knowledge base. However, some personality experts have argued that being more intelligent to begin with is what makes people more open rather than the other way around.

People who are open to new experiences are happier and more positive individuals and tend to have a better quality of life. They are curious and receptive to new ideas, which can certainly make them more agreeable and social. They are candid about their opinions, so you know where they stand on issues. Open individuals are less likely to deceive you or beat around the bush. They also tend to be flexible rather than closed-minded, making them more adaptable to change. Openness can be a great asset when dealing with stressful, uncertain situations.

**HOW OPEN ARE YOU?**

To estimate your level of openness, check off each of the following statements that describes you:

\_\_  I often come up with new ideas.

\_\_  I am curious about many things.

\_\_  I tend to be a deep thinker.

\_\_  People think I am a flexible person.

\_\_  I like doing creative things.

\_\_  I enjoy aesthetic experiences.

\_\_  My beliefs are unconventional.

\_\_  I don't enjoy routine tasks.

\_\_  I am good at tossing around new ideas.

\_\_  I have a lot of artistic interests.

If you checked five or more statements, you would likely score high on an openness scale. If you checked fewer statements, you are probably more on the closed end of the openness spectrum.

Parenting styles also vary according to a person's degree of openness. In studies of the interactions between parents and their children, mothers and fathers who score higher on the openness personality scale demonstrate greater warmth and empathy toward their children and tend to use nontraditional parenting strategies. They are also better at setting consistent and appropriate limits for their kids.

Like the other Big Five personality domains, openness to new experiences falls along a continuum. Consider where you might fall on the spectrum of closed versus open descriptors below. Many people have a combination of both closed and open traits, although some tend to land on one or the other end of the spectrum.

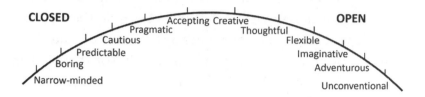

## CAN YOU BE TOO OPEN?

Openness is generally a positive personality trait. These imaginative and thoughtful individuals tend to be smarter, more flexible, and less likely to suffer from a mental disorder. But sometimes openness can have a downside.

Some open people may have a tendency to be too honest with others and "let it all hang out." That type of behavior can sometimes be hurtful and cruel and lead to social isolation.

Several years ago I treated Jenny, a talented young artist who had landed a job as an assistant curator at a prestigious art gallery. She needed the work to help make ends meet while establishing herself as a sculptor, and she was happy to have a job that connected her to the art world.

Jenny came in to see me because she was worried that she was going to be fired from the gallery. The manager had put her on notice because Jenny wasn't getting along with the other employees.

During Jenny's first few therapy sessions, we delved into what was going on at work, and she described how she dealt with people on the job.

"I'm basically an open and honest person, Dr. Small. I speak my mind if I have an opinion."

"How do your coworkers respond when you voice your opinions?" I asked.

"Some of them are so hypersensitive. They just can't take honesty, and then they talk about me behind my back."

For Jenny, her open and artistic nature contributed to her creativity, but those traits did not serve her well when it came to office politics. Her blunt comments were insulting and alienated her coworkers. It sounded like no one at work trusted her, and Jenny felt isolated at a job where collegial collaboration was an asset.

Even though each of the Big Five personality traits differs, many of them overlap. People who are open to new experiences also tend to be more extroverted, which is associated with greater popularity and social intelligence, but not always. Jenny was definitely extroverted, but her social intelligence was limited. She needed to learn some tact and understand how her "open and honest" attitude could be holding her back at the workplace. Jenny also needed some help in becoming more agreeable on the job.

I worked with Jenny in weekly psychotherapy over the next few months to help her gain a better perspective on the negative impact of her candor. At my suggestion, she tried role-playing with her sister to see how it felt when others criticized her, and that gave Jenny insight into how her personality style was hurtful to others. She came to realize that holding back on blurting out her opinions was not really "lying." Jenny discovered that it wasn't necessary to say every single thing she was thinking—it was a good idea to pause before speaking and consider the possible consequences of her words.

Although Jenny's psychotherapy only lasted a few months, it helped her adjust to and keep her job. She eventually left the gallery when her art career took off. Becoming more sensitive to the feelings of others helped her navigate the politics of the art world and get her sculptures to prospective buyers.

---

## DID YOU KNOW?

- Dog owners who score high in openness demonstrate greater emotional warmth toward their pets but less control over their pet's behavior.

- People who live on the East or West Coast score higher on an openness scale compared with those living in the Midwest or South.

- An open personality predicts greater susceptibility to a hypnotic trance.

- People who are open to new experiences are more likely to be politically liberal.

- By tracking Facebook likes from more than 58,000 volunteers, researchers were able to predict an individual's level of openness to the same rate of accuracy as a standard personality test.

---

Other aspects of openness can backfire as well. Some open individuals are overly receptive to new ideas and tend to be gullible. Whether it's a real estate scam or fake news, these people may be at higher risk for being victimized by scammers who take advantage of their receptive natures.

People who are too open can sometimes become overstimulated and distracted by too much information. Their openness can contribute to attention deficit challenges.

Being flexible certainly helps us adapt to stressful situations, but being too flexible can show a lack of commitment. Such open individuals may be viewed as self-serving and unwilling to speak out for their beliefs and values.

Some people who score high on openness are inclined toward distorted thinking and impulsivity, which can impair their social and professional relationships. Odd thinking and fantasizing are traits associated with excessive openness and characteristic of narcissistic and paranoid personality disorders.

Open individuals are more inclined to experiment with marijuana and other recreational drugs. In many places marijuana is legal, and people use it in moderation without negative effects. However, adolescents who use marijuana and other recreational drugs are at greater risk for negative health consequences.

---

## OPENNESS AND YOUR BRAIN

Thanks to international scientific collaborations that have amassed large brain scan databases, neuroscientists have revealed insights into how personality traits such as openness correlate with brain structure and function. In a 2016 paper published in the journal *Social Cognitive and Affective Neuroscience*, researchers focused on the anatomy of the outer brain surface known as the cortex. This is a large area with multiple folds where brain cells that control thinking, memory, and emotion reside. The investigators found that the openness personality trait was associated with reduced cortical thickness but increased area and folding in the frontal lobe (also known as the thinking brain). As the human brain evolved, it underwent a process called cortical stretching, which reduced the thickness of the cortex while increasing its area and number of folds so it could still fit within the skull. The findings from this study suggest that an individual who has a greater degree of openness to new experiences may have a more evolved brain. Other brain function studies indicate an association between openness and part of the frontal lobe that controls intelligence as well as the brain dopamine system, which helps modulate the brain's reward and pleasure centers.

## WHAT INFLUENCES OUR DEGREE OF OPENNESS?

As with other personality traits, inheritance plays a role in our tendency to be open. In studies of identical twins who share the exact same genes and DNA, researchers have discovered quite similar levels of openness. This holds true even for adopted identical twins who were separated at an early age and grew up with different families. One genetic study showed a significant association between openness and a specific form of a gene involved in transporting serotonin, an important brain messenger that controls a person's response to stressful life events.

As people age, their level of openness declines to some extent. In a study that drew upon survey data from more than 10,000 Americans, investigators found that with increasing age, an individual's willingness to be open to new experiences clearly diminishes.

A large investigation including more than 17,000 volunteers from 55 nations focused on personality differences between men and women. The scientists found minimal variances in openness among countries; however, these similarities did not hold for all nations. Sex-specific cultural roles and traditions likely have an influence on the openness personality trait.

Sexuality is also related to openness. It's not surprising that both men and women who have stronger sex drives as well as more liberal attitudes about sex are more likely to score high on an openness assessment.

A person's susceptibility to hypnosis is also associated with that individual's degree of openness. People open to new experiences can readily focus their full attention, become absorbed under the hypnotist's guidance, and quickly go into a trance. That same capacity assists an open person to focus attention on problem solving and original thinking, which contributes to creativity and intellectual curiosity.

## OPEN VERSUS CLOSED PERSONALITIES: TYPICAL TRAITS

| Open | Closed |
|------|--------|
| Adventurous | Accepting |
| Creative | Cautious |
| Imaginative | Conventional |
| Inquisitive | Inattentive |
| Original | Pragmatic |
| Thoughtful | Predictable |
| Unconventional | Traditional |

## STRATEGIES FOR BECOMING MORE OPEN

Although too much openness can get some people into trouble, in general being open to new experiences has many benefits. If you tend to be too cautious, predictable, or fearful of new things and you'd like to enjoy the excitement of novelty and greater openness, consider some of the following strategies to help you open up and expand your horizons.

- *Learn to listen.* Closed-off individuals often appear as know-it-alls. When they constantly voice their opinions, they don't give themselves a chance to take note of other people's points of view. Make a concerted effort to slow yourself down and consciously listen to what others have to say. Even if you don't completely agree with their viewpoint or opinions, there may be an element of truth that makes sense to you. Accept that you can't possibly be right about everything and that there may be other points of view worth considering.
- *Be honest.* People who are closed off to new experiences often rationalize their attitudes and actions and fail to

voice their true opinions to others. Having an open mind means reassessing some of your underlying assumptions about yourself and others.

- *Ask questions.* When we're closed off, we tend to tell others how we see the world without bothering to take in their views. Make an effort to ask others about themselves, how they are feeling, and what they are thinking. When they respond, try to listen closely to their comments in order to allow a true exchange of ideas.

- *Practice letting go.* Fear of the unknown motivates many people to keep tight control over everything in their lives. Planning ahead can certainly diminish future uncertainties and manage fear of the unknown, but when we're always in control, we can miss opportunities to open our minds to new experiences and ideas. Try taking baby steps to give up control in some aspect of your life. For instance, if you insist on always driving when you're with others, try letting someone else take the wheel for a short trip. Once you become comfortable riding, you can enjoy being chauffeured for longer outings. Generally letting go of your need to control things will open you up to new ideas and experiences.

- *Step out of your routine.* Many people fear change because they worry about physical danger, psychological harm, or both. They may develop daily habits that make their lives feel safer and more efficient, but those routines can close them off from exploring novel ideas and experiences. Consider eating at a new restaurant, trying a new sport, or taking a vacation to somewhere you've never been. Try to shake up your routine, even just a little, to help open yourself to innovative concepts and options that may enrich your life and expand your mind.

- *Expect mistakes.* When we change our routines and venture into new and unfamiliar territory, we may stumble or make errors. Allow yourself to make mistakes and forgive yourself when you do so. More important, try to learn from those missteps and move forward.

- *Become mindful.* Thanks to today's technology boom, many of us are bombarded by too much information and continual distraction from our gadgets. All those texts, instant messages, emails, and other incoming data can divert our minds from what's happening in the moment. Slow yourself down, stop texting, and give your Facebook page a rest so you can become more mindful in the here and now. Consider meditation, Tai Chi, yoga, or other relaxation techniques to help open your mind to new ideas and experiences.

- *Get creative.* Consider taking an art class or attending a music appreciation workshop. If you learned to play the piano as a child, you may want to dust off those ivories and fire up your musical neural circuits. Creative pursuits open our minds to new ideas, which in turn exercise our brains and often bring about tremendous pleasure.

# CHAPTER 9

## Fast-Tracking Your Change with Therapy

*I told my psychiatrist that everyone hates me.*
*He said I was being ridiculous—everyone hasn't*
*met me yet.*

—Rodney Dangerfield

**THERE ARE MANY PATHS** to achieving meaningful change, and the better you know yourself before you begin, the easier it will be to discover the path that's right for you. Some self-sufficient people prefer the do-it-yourself approach with self-help strategies. Others may achieve their desired changes faster with the help of a therapist or counselor guiding them along their course of change. Still others find that a combination of self-help strategies and professional assistance is the most effective way to reach their goals.

If you believe that your goals are achievable and you are comfortable going it alone, then starting with do-it-yourself strategies makes sense as an initial approach. However, if your problems are pressing, severe, or disruptive to your daily life, seeking professional help may be a more prudent option.

Finding the right therapist involves a certain amount of self-knowledge and understanding of your options. If you already know that you have a diagnosis of depression or bipolar disorder, it would behoove you to find a psychiatrist with expertise in mood disorders and medication treatments. If you don't need such specialized medical approaches, you might do fine with a psychologist or social worker.

Many people are aware that they have issues, but they have never gotten a specific diagnosis. Their starting point would involve seeking a clinician who can help them better understand the nature of their problems and point them toward an appropriate treatment and therapist. Keep in mind that as people learn more about themselves and make progress in therapy, the type of doctor or counselor that is most appropriate for them may change as well.

Cultural and geographic norms can influence an individual's openness to working with a therapist. In many parts of the world, psychiatrists and psychologists are just not available or their services are shunned or even feared. In other regions, therapy is extremely popular and even fashionable. Such local attitudes often influence a person's acceptance or reluctance to see a therapist.

---

### DID YOU KNOW?

- According to the American Psychological Association state licensing board, California, New York, and Pennsylvania have the most licensed psychologists, while Wyoming, South Dakota, and Alaska have the fewest.

- Argentina has the highest number of psychologists per capita in the world, with nearly 200 psychologists per 100,000 residents.

This chapter will examine some of the key considerations to keep in mind when looking for a therapist. That way you can avoid the pitfalls of working with someone who is not a good fit for your current personality and less likely to help you achieve the meaningful change you desire.

## TYPES OF THERAPISTS

Good therapists share several personal attributes. They generally like doing therapy and enjoy their jobs. They also tend to have a positive outlook and convey an optimistic view of the world. Effective therapists are skilled communicators—they make their clients feel understood. Most good mental health professionals are also eager detectives. They want to discover what leads clients to think, feel, and do what they do in order to figure out the best way to help. Warmth and a sense of humor also help therapists connect with their clients and establish a collaborative relationship. Being honest and ethical are other critical traits that a good therapist will possess.

These are all important attributes to look for in any therapist you choose, but you will also need to hone in on the type of professional who is best for your current needs. If you search online or open up a phone directory, you will find an alphabet soup of degrees and titles for various types of counselors and therapists. To help you understand the differences among these professionals, the following includes brief descriptions of various mental health professionals who provide talk therapies and other kinds of interventions.

*Psychiatrists.* After graduating medical school with a medical degree (MD), these doctors spend another four years training in general psychiatry. Psychiatrists are taught to do psychotherapy (i.e., talk therapy) as well as medication treatment. Some develop skills in more specialized medical treatments, such as electroconvulsive therapy or transmag-netic stimulation. For someone with a mental disorder such as major depression, bipolar disorder, panic disorder, obsessive-compulsive disorder or any mental health problem requir-ing medicines or medical treatments, a psychiatrist is often needed but not always necessary. For example, some patients receive their antidepressant prescriptions from their internist or family doctor and obtain psychological counseling from a non-MD psychotherapist.

*Psychologists.* These professionals attend psychology gradu-ate school where they receive either a PhD (doctor of philoso-phy in psychology) or PsyD (doctor of psychology) degree in psychology. In addition to learning about the human mind and behavior, they obtain training in counseling, psychotherapy, and psychological testing, which can assist in diagnosing men-tal problems.

*Social workers.* These professionals usually obtain a master of social work (MSW) degree as well as clinical training to provide social services, often in health care settings. They fre-quently assist clients who are economically, physically, mentally, or socially disadvantaged. Many social workers also offer coun-seling and psychotherapy.

*Licensed professional counselors.* These counselors obtain a state license after completing a master degree (often a marriage, family, child counselor or MFCC) and additional clinical train-ing. They perform individual, family, and couples therapy for a range of emotional and relationship problems.

*Psychoanalysts.* These are psychiatrists, psychologists, or other mental health professionals who obtain advanced training in psychoanalysis. They offer an intensive form of therapy that aims to uncover the patient's unconscious conflicts in order to provide insights that relieve psychological symptoms.

## VARIOUS PSYCHOTHERAPY METHODS: ONE SIZE DOESN'T FIT ALL

In addition to training and educational background, your choice of a therapist will depend on the clinician's area of expertise and the type of psychotherapy that is likely to be effective for you. If you have the capacity for self-reflection and introspection, you may very well benefit from insight-oriented or psychodynamic therapy, which explores inner motivations for behaviors. A more action-oriented person might prefer behavioral therapy, which enlightens clients about their reactions to stimuli that trigger their unwanted behaviors.

Several years ago, a pharmaceutical sales rep named Susan sought my help after being in insight-oriented psychodynamic therapy for more than a year. She was not a very introspective person, and her therapist gave her very little direction except to explore what she was feeling and thinking. Susan found that her symptoms were not getting better, and she wanted to try a different approach. Because of her action-oriented personality, I decided to use a cognitive behavioral therapeutic strategy with her. We set short-term goals and focused on practical problem-solving techniques for her present-day conflicts. She was much more comfortable with this therapeutic style than the more open-ended exploratory treatment, and her symptoms improved quickly.

These kinds of individual preferences are important to consider when opting for therapy. The systematic research demonstrating that therapy can change personality, however, has shown that on average, the specific type of therapy may not matter as much as the individual qualities of the therapist.

## SOME POPULAR FORMS OF PSYCHOTHERAPY

- *Cognitive behavioral therapy* helps people develop new ways of thinking by identifying and altering their perceptions about themselves and others.

- *Psychodynamic therapy* helps people understand their unresolved and often unconscious conflicts that sometimes go back to childhood in order to cope better with their feelings.

- *Supportive psychotherapy* assists clients in expressing themselves and reduces their emotional distress through advice, encouragement, and reassurance.

- *Interpersonal therapy* aims to improve communication skills and self-esteem by focusing on the client's behaviors and interactions with family members and friends.

- *Dialectical behavior therapy* can help patients with personality disorders change their unhealthy behaviors into healthy ones by keeping daily diaries and engaging in phone, individual, and group therapy.

- *Eclectic, integrative, or holistic therapy* blends elements of various therapeutic approaches and tailors the treatment to the client's particular needs.

Some people who wish to change their personalities also suffer from mental disorders, and knowledge of their specific psychological issues and baseline personality traits will help guide them toward the most effective type of therapy for change. A person with a high level of neuroticism and a panic disorder might do well with cognitive behavioral therapy, which would help that individual gain some emotional stability as well as control over their panic attacks. An introspective, shy person who wishes to become more extroverted might do well with a psychodynamic therapeutic approach.

Most psychotherapy is provided individually through one-on-one sessions between the client and the therapist, but other formats can also be effective depending on an individual's problems and preferences. If marital issues seem to be fueling negative personality traits, then couples therapy may be the best option. People with addictive personalities can overcome their self-destructive behaviors through group therapy with other substance abusers, who may offer emotional support and practical solutions to their everyday challenges. Working together with close relatives in family therapy can help family members with their relationships and lead to meaningful change for several of them. For people in rural areas where therapists are sparse, online options can be convenient and effective. Some people like to use the internet, video chat, or the telephone to augment their face-to-face therapy sessions.

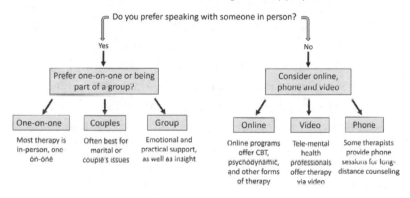

Considerations When Choosing a Therapy Option

Do you prefer speaking with someone in person?

## OVERCOMING FEAR OF THERAPY

Many people have a tremendous fear of psychotherapy. It's remarkable that many individuals spend years and years studying a variety of topics in school, yet the idea of studying themselves is the last thing that they would consider. Much of this kind of resistance to therapy stems from anxiety about what may really be bothering them. They often fear that therapy will uncover some dark, deep secret that could unleash psychological havoc and make their problems worse.

There are individuals who fear therapy because they worry that it will somehow completely change who they are. Artists, writers, and other imaginative individuals sometimes describe how their creative juices flow when they experience angst and psychological discomfort. They believe that therapy will remove their inner conflicts and stifle their creative edge.

Some individuals are too ashamed about their problems to seek help, while others are reluctant to begin therapy because of social anxiety. People who are shy and introverted may become uncomfortable when meeting new people. Their level of discomfort gets even worse if they believe that the person they are meeting will learn about the most personal details of their lives.

For some people, their excuse for avoiding therapy is based on the belief that talking to a therapist about their inner secrets will put them at risk for public exposure or legal problems. However, all ethical therapists abide by strict confidentiality rules. They agree to keep the client's information confidential, just as an attorney would with any client, unless of course the patient reveals information that puts them or someone else in immediate danger. In other words, your therapy sessions are completely confidential unless you reveal serious suicidal or homicidal plans.

Other people shun therapy because they believe that therapists don't really care about their clients. They are under the false impression that they can get more accomplished by just talking to a friend about what's bothering them. Certainly sharing your worries with an empathic friend can be therapeutic, but even our most empathic friends have their own interests that may conflict with ours and get in the way of psychological help.

The usual agreement in a therapeutic relationship is that the client pays for the therapist's time and expertise, and in exchange, the therapist focuses on the patient's needs and not their own. Effective counselors do care about their clients in a real way, but their concern is detached enough to prevent them from getting overly involved in their client's problems. That detached concern allows them to be more objective and helpful than a friend who may have his or her own personal agenda in the relationship.

---

## TOP 10 PSYCHOTHERAPY MYTHS

1. Only crazy people see therapists.

2. Psychotherapy will rob me of my creativity.

3. Therapists can't be trusted because they tell their friends about your problems.

4. Psychotherapy takes too long and costs too much money to do any good.

5. A therapist is just a paid friend.

6. Therapists try to make you dependent on them.

7. Talking about my childhood can't solve my problems.

8. Therapy will change who I really am.

9. All therapists talk in psychobabble.

10. Seeing a therapist means that I am a weak person.

---

Most fears people have about therapy are based on unfounded assumptions. People often avoid therapy because they are unable to admit they have a problem or they embrace a stigma about "seeing a shrink." Fueled in part by the media, there exists an unjustified pessimism about psychotherapy that discourages some people from getting the help they need.

Overcoming the fear of therapy involves having the courage to admit to our own weaknesses and the motivation to do something about them. The best way to move beyond such an impasse is to make the effort to become informed and accept that the myths about psychotherapy stem from unfounded assumptions based on ignorance. The truth is that most professionals who practice psychotherapy are caring, ethical, and helpful individuals. Meeting the right counselor for you and discovering how talk therapy can help you change is the most effective way to overcome the fear of therapy.

## CHEMISTRY COUNTS

In trying to decide on the right therapist, you might come up with a list of the most important qualities you are seeking in a counselor, such as their therapy style, age, background, and other professional qualities. Keep in mind that even if you find a potential therapist that meets your qualifications and sounds good on the telephone, the two of you may not click when you meet in person.

A therapeutic relationship should never be a romantic relationship, although the process of picking the right therapist can feel a bit like dating. Some of the same instincts people rely on when they're dating can be informative about whether or not the therapeutic relationship will work. People often attribute those subtle interactions and the feelings they evoke to chemistry, which can predict whether a therapist and client can work well together.

In psychoanalysis and in-depth psychodynamic therapy, the patient does sometimes experience romantic feelings toward the therapist. But those feelings are revealed and explored as part of the therapeutic process. The patient comes to understand how the feelings are distortions, which can provide insights into the patient's other relationships outside of therapy.

A preference for a male or female therapist can be import-ant as well. It often stems from the person's prior relationships with parents and siblings. I once treated a female graduate student who had control issues but mostly with other women. Her mother had been overbearing, while her father had been the parent she always turned to for emotional support. This patient's past history of confiding in an older man, her father, made her comfortable talking candidly with me about her unre-solved childhood resentments toward her mother. Had she seen a female therapist, she might have struggled more in therapy because she may have perceived the therapist as too controlling like her mother.

If you and your prospective therapist have similar back-grounds, interests, and values, the likelihood of compatibility will be greater. But an effective therapeutic relationship depends on other qualities as well. For example, you may find it taxing to spend time with people who don't share your sense of humor, and if your therapist is humorless, it may be hard for the two of you to connect. Humor can be emotionally healing when used effectively in therapy, and it provides a way to gain perspective on uncomfortable feelings.

Many relationships, whether social or therapeutic, strengthen over time as mutual trust builds. Early on in your therapy, you will observe your therapist and how she operates, which will hopefully help you develop trust. Does your therapist behave in a professional manner? Is she a good listener? Does she follow up on what she says she will do? If your therapist turns out to be unpredictable and inconsistent, it will be hard to develop trust.

Because therapy and counseling are helping professions, most therapists tend to be kind and caring. However, a therapist who is too nice may not be the most therapeutic. Sometimes setting limits and practicing a little "tough love" is essential for helping a client resolve psychological conflicts and achieve personal growth.

It's normal to feel a bit anxious when you begin therapy, but if your therapist is making you feel excessively anxious, this person may not be a good fit for you. You are attempting to get to know someone who is going to learn quite a lot about you. It's also important to be aware of any red flags that may inform you that a therapist is not right for you.

---

### RED FLAGS THAT YOU SHOULD AVOID A PARTICULAR THERAPIST

Therapists are human beings, so none of them is perfect. However, if you notice any of the following in your prospective therapist, it's time to move on:

- Inappropriate touching, hugging, joking
- Offering up too much personal information
- Inattentiveness and distraction during sessions (e.g., answering the phone, watching the clock, checking email)
- Overly critical and insulting remarks
- Revealing details about other clients

---

## THERAPIST SHOPPING

One of the best ways to find a therapist is to ask for referrals from people you trust. Primary care doctors observe a lot of psychological problems in their patients, and they often work with psychiatrists, psychologists, and other mental health professionals to help them manage those problems. If you trust your internist or family physician, that's a good place to start asking for a referral. If you happen to be friends with someone in the mental health field, that person would be an excellent referral source too. However, even though you may trust that therapist friend quite a bit, it's important not to have a friend become your therapist. Not only will you end up damaging the friendship; your therapist friend would likely have challenges in remaining objective in the therapy as well. An ethical counselor never treats friends or family members.

Friends and relatives who have been in their own therapy can be excellent referral sources. Chances are they went through their own vetting process to find their therapist, and they may be able to enlighten you about who's out there and who might be a good match for you. Many friends will offer to check with their own therapists to help you with referrals.

Another important referral source is a local university medical center department of psychiatry or psychology. Mental health professionals affiliated with reputable academic medical centers are generally accomplished individuals with excellent credentials and experience. Local or national branches of professional societies as well as national advocacy organizations can also be helpful referral sources. Members of these groups agree to professional and ethical standards set by the organizations, which also offer continuing education to their members.

## YOUR THERAPY PRIORITIES

Some people never bother to find a therapist because they become overwhelmed by all the considerations and they don't know where to begin. To avoid this kind of mental exhaustion, make a list of your priorities when it comes to the qualities of the therapist and the type of therapy you desire. Once you have a list of what's important to you, it will be easier to navigate your many options.

## ORGANIZATIONS THAT CAN HELP YOU FIND A THERAPIST

The websites of the following organizations include links that can guide you to therapists in your area:

- *American Psychiatric Association* (www.psychiatry.org). A medical specialty society that works to ensure effective treatment of mental disorders.

- *American Psychological Association* (www.apa.org). An organization that represents US psychologists and promotes health, education, and human welfare.

- *American Academy of Psychotherapists* (www.aapweb.com). A multidisciplinary community of psychotherapists that aims to invigorate and support the psychotherapist's quest for excellence.

- *American Association for Geriatric Psychiatry* (www.aagponline.org). A professional organization dedicated to enhancing the mental health and well-being of older adults through education and research.

- *American Counseling Association* (www.counseling.org). The largest association representing professional counselors in various settings.

- *Anxiety and Depression Association of America* (www.aada.org). An international nonprofit association focusing on education, training, and research.

- *Mental Health America* (www.mentalhealthamerica.net). A national community-based nonprofit organization dedicated to addressing mental illness needs.

- *National Alliance of Mental Illness* (www.nami.org). The nation's largest grassroots mental health advocacy group.

- *National Association of Social Workers* (www.naswdc.org). The leading membership organization of professional social workers.

While discussing therapy referrals with people, try to find out about any practical considerations that may be important, especially insurance needs, preferred geographic location, and any preferences regarding personal qualities of the therapist. Given the many barriers to therapy and the resistance of so many people, eliminating practical roadblocks can be critical for getting people started.

Randy, an old friend of mine, was particularly conscientious and wanted to become more extroverted, so he asked me for a psychotherapy referral. Thanks to his conscientious nature, Randy presented the following list of requirements to me:

1. Middle-aged male
2. West side of town
3. Accepts health insurance
4. Cognitive behavioral therapy expert
5. Available for weekend appointments

Randy's priorities were straightforward and practical, which made it easier for me to come up with some recommendations that could guide him to the right therapist. And when I do make recommendations, I usually provide several names so the person can have more than one option.

When you first speak with your potential therapist on the phone, feel free to ask direct questions about credentials. Asking about prior training, areas of expertise, and professional fees are all fair game. You may not find out everything during the initial phone conversation, so feel free to ask more questions during your first appointment.

Don't expect to learn much about the therapist's personal life. Psychotherapy is about you and not about the therapist. Knowing too much personal information about your therapist can be distracting from your therapeutic work, and any counselor who offers up detailed information about themselves may have issues in maintaining appropriate therapeutic boundaries. That person is probably not the ethical practitioner you are looking for.

Early in the course of therapy, you and your therapist should get clear on the goals of your treatment. Just sitting down and talking about what's bothering you without specific goals in mind could lead to a therapeutic relationship that has no end in sight. If someone walked in on any of your therapy sessions (which hopefully never happens) and asked each of you about your therapeutic goals, ideally you would both give the same answer.

These practical priorities are important to consider, but always keep in mind that chemistry counts. If you don't feel comfortable working with a particular individual, it is your prerogative to find someone else who may be a better fit. But don't be too quick to change therapists. It could be that your counselor is probing in an area of your life that you find uncomfortable, but delving a little deeper into some of your issues may provide insights that help you change for the better in the long run.

# CHAPTER 10

---

# 30 Days to a Better You

---

*The secret of change is to focus all of your energy,*
*not on fighting the old, but on building the new.*
—Dan Millman

**I** **ORIGINALLY BECAME A PSYCHIATRIST** because of my fascination with the mind and human behavior as well as my wish to help people change for the better. Now after decades of research and practice, I know very well that unless someone is highly motivated and ready for change, no therapist can be of much help. However, if you are sufficiently motivated and committed to making a change, then you have moved beyond the considering phase and are now ready to devise your plan.

In the preceding chapters, we discussed the science of personality change as well as many of the strategies that have been shown to help people alter their lives for the better. This chapter will help you map out your personalized plan for achieving your goals and move you smoothly through the CPAS phases of change—considering, planning, acting, and sustaining.

Once you begin taking action, the scientific evidence suggests that you can achieve meaningful change after just one month.

You will also be able to lean on the CPAS method for maintaining those change benefits for the rest of your life. Keep in mind, however, that lapses may occur now and then. But don't worry—if you do experience a setback, you will have the tools to rapidly bounce back to your new, improved self. The following diagram outlines the key CPAS phases leading to meaningful personality change.

## Key Steps to Changing Your Personality

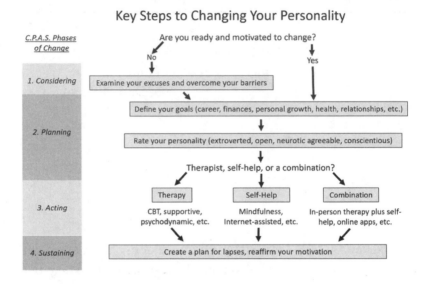

ARE YOU READY TO CHANGE?

Beth was a 31-year-old high school teacher who was considering a change in her life. She'd been living with her boyfriend Ethan for the previous three years and was eager to start a family, but he was not interested in having children. They had tried couples therapy, but no one was willing to budge. Beth knew that if she were ever going to have kids, she would need to do something proactive, and it probably wouldn't involve staying with Ethan. She had been thinking about leaving him, but she wasn't quite ready.

To help her move beyond the considering phase, I recommended that Beth create a list with two columns: the left-hand column included the changes she wished to achieve, and on the right side, she listed her excuses for not doing them.

## BETH'S LIST OF THE GOALS SHE'D LIKE TO ACHIEVE
## AND HER EXCUSES FOR NOT DOING THEM

| I want to | I can't because |
|---|---|
| 1. have a relationship with someone who also wants children, | 1. I know Ethan loves me and I will be lonely if I break it off, |
| 2. give Ethan an ultimatum and tell him to move out, | 2. I hate confrontations–he'll eventually get the idea and move, |
| 3. get out and meet people with similar interests. | 3. it's too much work to meet new people and date. |
| 4. | 4. |
| 5. | 5. |
| 6. | 6. |

Although Beth felt stuck in the considering phase, this exercise began to give her some insight. Try it for yourself. Below is a template to help you create your own list of what you want to change and why you may believe you can't.

## WHAT I WANT AND WHY I CAN'T

| I want to | I can't because |
|---|---|
| 1. | 1. |
| 2. | 2. |
| 3. | 3. |
| 4. | 4. |
| 5. | 5. |
| 6. | 6. |

When Beth saw the two columns in black and white, she recognized that a lot of her excuses for not changing were simply old ways of thinking and habits that no longer worked in her life. Beth was admittedly a loner and always had difficulty meeting new people. She was also agreeable to a fault, which meant that she avoided all confrontations, even ones that could move her toward her goals.

Beth's first step was to let go of her excuses and self-inflicted barriers to change and muster the motivation she needed to move forward. She found that by combining certain self-help strategies with a bit of psychotherapy, she was able to adjust the personality traits that were holding her back and change her life for the better.

Many people face self-inflicted barriers to change including old, counterproductive habits; toxic relationships; or the misguided belief that it's impossible to change. Beth told me that one of her barriers was her best friend from high school, Renee. Renee really liked Ethan and constantly discouraged Beth from breaking off the relationship. In our psychotherapy sessions, Beth was able to recognize that Renee had her own agenda—Renee couldn't have kids, and she probably didn't want to lose Beth to a bunch of diapers and mommy-and-me classes. Gaining this insight about her friend removed another one of Beth's barriers and boosted her emotional strength and motivation.

## THE PLANNING PHASE

Once you've fortified your motivation and overcome your barriers, you will be ready to move on to the planning phase. This phase involves three important steps:

1. *Review your baseline personality.* Recheck your current personality trait scores in chapter 3 to help guide you toward which personality traits you wish to change.
2. *Define your goals.* Begin with large strokes, big-picture objectives such as improving personal health, professional life, relationships, wellness, or some other area of concern, and then focus in on your specific aims.
3. *Decide on your preferred method for change.* Determine whether you are interested in a self-help approach, working with a therapist, or a combination of the two.

## MATCH YOUR GOALS WITH THE PERSONALITY YOU DESIRE

Now that Beth was in the planning phase, she focused on her number one goal: to get married and have children. She was very motivated, partly because of her age and what she believed were her limited number of child-bearing years left. In her personality assessment, Beth scored high on agreeableness and low on extraversion. To achieve her goal, she would need to become (1) *less agreeable* so she could confront her boyfriend about moving out and (2) *more extroverted* to allow her to start dating and hopefully find someone with similar values and plans.

Beth's high agreeableness score would normally be considered a positive trait. However, in her case, Beth had to become a bit more disagreeable in order to break up with her boyfriend. Below are other examples of how people can match up their goals with their desired personality traits.

## ALIGNING YOUR GOALS WITH YOUR DESIRED PERSONALITY

| Goals | | Desired Personality Change |
|---|---|---|
| Overcome fear of conflict; become less gullible; develop creative side | → | Less agreeable |
| Be more considerate and trusting; improve friendships; resolve marital difficulties | → | More agreeable |
| Achieve personal growth, better relationships; become more self-confident, calmer | → | Less neurotic |
| Better social life, career success; overcome shyness; become more assertive | → | More extroverted |
| Become more thoughtful, more laid-back, and less reckless | → | Less extroverted |
| Become more adventurous; expand social life; develop a creative side | → | More open |
| Achieve greater career success; improve relationships | → | More conscientious |

Because you may have achieved some change already just by reading this book, reassess where you stand in the Big Five personality traits by using the "Rate Your Current Personality" assessment tool in chapter 3. Then enter your scores below.

---

## YOUR BIG FIVE PERSONALITY SCORES

For each of the Big Five categories, enter your score (ranging from 7 to 35) in the boxes below:

- Extraversion score: _____

- Openness score: _____

- Emotional stability score: _____

- Agreeableness score: _____

- Conscientiousness score: _____

A low-ranging score in any of these categories would be between 7 and 21, while a high-ranging score would be between 22 and 35.

---

Also, take another look at the goals you originally defined in chapter 3. You may wish to fine-tune some of your objectives. Prioritize your goals and desired personality traits below.

| Goals | | Desired Personality Change |
|---|---|---|
| | → | |
| | → | |
| | → | |
| | → | |
| | → | |

With your number one goal in mind, consider the personality adjustments that make sense for achieving that goal. If your aim is to get a job promotion and your conscientiousness score is in the low range, then you may want to become more conscientious. If you feel alone or isolated and you scored low on the extraversion scale, your desired personality change might be increased extraversion. However, if your social isolation is due to a tendency to be argumentative and pushy, you probably scored low on agreeableness and need to pump up that personality trait.

The final step in your planning phase is to decide whether you want to proceed on your own, get help from a counselor or therapist, or combine both approaches. If your issues seem daunting, you might lean toward getting help from a therapist. If you are more of a self-starter, then do-it-yourself approaches could be your initial strategy. All these methods have been shown to help people achieve meaningful change, and several types of interventions—from cognitive behavioral therapy to mindfulness meditation—are accessible online and through downloadable apps.

Because I had helped Beth work through her considering phase and overcome her barriers to change, she was already comfortable with counseling and wanted to return to therapy with me to work on her objectives of becoming less agreeable and more extroverted. One of Beth's greatest motivators was her biological clock ticking. She wanted to double down on her efforts, so we began meeting for therapy twice a week. My plan was to use an eclectic therapeutic strategy, combining insight-oriented approaches with some cognitive behavioral techniques.

To help you decide whether to begin with a psychotherapist or a self-help method, check off the statements below that apply to you.

- I am a self-starter and usually don't need outside encouragement to motivate me.
- My goals seem achievable.

- My psychological issues are minimal.
- I've done well in the past with self-help strategies.
- I don't have time to go to a therapist.

If you find that several of the above statements ring true for you, then you may want to begin by trying do-it-yourself approaches. By contrast, if any of the statements below describe you better, then I recommend starting with a professional counselor or therapist:

- My goals seem daunting.
- I have trouble getting motivated without support from others.
- My psychological issues seem to have a big impact on my everyday life.
- I have a major psychiatric illness and need medication to treat it.
- Psychotherapy has helped me in the past.

If you are sitting on the fence about whether to go it alone or enlist a counselor's help, my suggestion is to begin with some guidance from a professional. You can also incorporate self-help approaches to augment your therapy or even shift to a fully do-it-yourself strategy later on.

There are several common therapeutic approaches to choose from, including the following:

- *Cognitive behavioral therapy.* Assists clients to think differently and encourages healthier perceptions and behaviors.
- *Psychodynamic therapy.* Provides clients with a greater understanding of their unresolved conflicts so they can cope better with their feelings.
- *Supportive psychotherapy.* Reduces emotional distress through advice, encouragement, and reassurance.

- *Interpersonal therapy.* Focuses on the client's behaviors and interactions with others to improve communication skills and self-esteem.
- *Eclectic, integrative or holistic therapy.* A blend of various approaches that is tailored to the client's particular needs.

If you do decide to engage a therapist, one size does not fit all, and you will want to choose a professional that fits with your needs. Each type of therapist has different educational backgrounds, areas of expertise, and forms of services offered.

---

### TYPES OF THERAPISTS TO CHOOSE FROM

- *Psychiatrist*–MD degree; provides diagnostic services as well as medication and talk therapy

- *Psychologist*–PhD or PsyD; diagnosis, psychotherapy, psychological testing

- *Social worker*–MSW; counseling, support, focus on disadvantaged clients

- *Licensed professional counselor*–MFCC; support, counseling

- *Psychoanalyst*–intensive psychotherapy to resolve psychological conflicts

---

The form of therapy you feel will work best for you should partly determine which type of professional you choose. For example, if you feel cognitive behavioral therapy is the right approach, then a psychologist with experience in CBT may be your best choice. If you need medication treatment, then a psychiatrist would make sense.

## IMPORTANT CONSIDERATIONS WHEN CHOOSING A THERAPIST

- *Referrals.* Trustworthy friends, relatives, doctors, or others can recommend a therapist, and you can also obtain referrals from national organizations and local, well-respected health systems.

- *Personal preferences.* The therapist's age, background, and education may be important to you.

- *Practical issues.* Location, availability, insurance, and fees should be considered.

- *Chemistry.* Remain mindful of your instincts about the therapist and whether or not the two of you "click."

- *Red flags.* Avoid therapists who seem inappropriate, inattentive, or overly critical.

If you decide to begin your program for change with self-help approaches, you'll first need to explore the various products and programs available. There are several online programs and apps that provide cognitive behavioral techniques as well as mindfulness meditation and relaxation methods. Some also offer psychodynamic therapy.

## ONLINE RESOURCES

The following are examples of apps and online resources that can help you improve your personality using do-it-yourself strategies. Although most apps and internet programs have not undergone systematic controlled research, they still apply the general principles of the particular strategy you have chosen to reach your goals. To explore these programs, search your app store or the internet using the program's name or a related search term.

| Therapeutic Strategy or Goal | Key Word to App or Site |
|---|---|
| Cognitive behavioral therapy | Anxiety Coach, iCouch, iCounselor, MoodKit, MoodLytics, Thought Diary Pro |
| Combined supportive, educational journaling | iMoodJournal, Moody Me, MindShift, Pacifica, Stress & Anxiety Companion, SuperBetter |
| Psychodynamic, supportive therapy | Breakthrough.com, Doctor on Demand, Heal Yourself with Psychotherapy, Talk Space |
| Stress reduction, meditation | BellyBio, Calm, HeadSpace, In Hand, Insight Timer, Stop, Breathe & Think |
| Better sleep | iSleepEasy, Rain Sleep Sounds, SHUTi, Sleepio, White Noise |
| Health, fitness, weight management | Cyclemeter, FitBit, Lose It, MyFitnessPal, Runmeter, Therapy Buddy, Weight Watchers |

## TAKING ACTION

Congratulations on getting this far. You have overcome your barriers to change and accepted that some of your reasons for doing nothing were just excuses for continuing old, useless behaviors and avoiding the temporary discomfort of change. You have defined your goals and identified the behaviors and personality traits you wish to change. You have also decided on whether to move forward on your own, with the help of a therapist, or a combination of the two.

Your plan is in place and you're ready to begin the acting phase. If you stay the course for the next 30 days, there is a very good chance that you will experience meaningful improvements in your life. You'll start letting go of the uncomfortable thoughts and feelings that have been holding you back and begin adopting new and healthier behaviors.

Once Beth and I started meeting twice weekly, she made swift progress toward changing her personality and improving her life. In the first two sessions, we explored her fears about confrontation. Beth recalled that as a child, she had been afraid to confront her mother, even though her mom constantly disappointed her and never followed through on her promises. Beth was able to make the connection between those fearful childhood feelings and how they still dictated her adult behavior—especially with Ethan. She soon realized that although Ethan was disappointing her by not wanting a family, she was an adult now and Ethan was *not* her mother. She rallied the courage to confront him, but her friend Renee intervened and talked her out of it.

Beth and I spent the next session reviewing her motivations for change and how important having her own family was to her. We discussed her plan to become less agreeable and more extroverted. Afterward she was once again determined to ignore Renee's advice and confront Ethan.

By the end of the second week of therapy, Beth sat Ethan down and gave him an ultimatum—either agree to have a child or move out. The confrontation was easier than Beth had anticipated. It was upsetting, but no one yelled or threw any dishes. For a moment, she thought that Ethan might come around, but then he said he understood what Beth wanted and knew that he couldn't give it to her. He agreed to look for a place, and in a week he moved out. Beth felt sad when Ethan handed her his house key, but she was also tremendously relieved.

We spent the next few sessions focusing on cognitive behavioral strategies to help Beth become more outgoing and comfortable when meeting new people. She decided to supplement her therapy sessions with some internet-based CBT, and by the end of the month, she was dating again. This time she vowed not to waste time on men who had no interest in having a family. I also suggested that Beth try some mindfulness practices to help overcome her anxiety about meeting new people. She downloaded a meditation app on her smartphone and began attending a weekly yoga class. These relaxation exercises helped Beth feel calmer and more confident.

---

### BETH'S COGNITIVE BEHAVIORAL STRATEGIES

- *Become aware of negative distortions.* Beth caught herself whenever her old, familiar negative thoughts reemerged. If she heard her inner voice say, "You'll never meet anyone as great as Ethan" or "There's no way you can just approach that guy and start up a conversation," she would recognize them as false and sabotaging patterns from her past.

- *Entertain new ways of thinking.* After each negative prediction, Beth began asking herself, "How else could I think about this?" She practiced putting her negative thinking into perspective by considering three possible outcomes: (1) the worst possible result, (2) the best thing that could happen, and (3) the most realistic outcome.

- *Test out your new thoughts and behaviors.* Although Beth remained a little on the shy side, she was able to start going out with friends and meeting new people. A guy she knew from work asked her out on a date, and Beth took the plunge. It turned out that he wasn't a complete loser (worst outcome) or the love of her life (best outcome) but someone who was interesting and whom she'd like to see again (realistic outcome).

Each person's acting phase will differ depending on their particular goals and desired personality changes. For example, David was a 25-year-old graduate student who sometimes suffered crippling anxiety due to the pressures of his PhD program. His personality assessment indicated low scores on emotional stability, and he needed help in reducing his anxiety. David found a psychologist with expertise in worry-exposure therapy.

The scientific evidence indicates that for people like David who wish to tame their neuroses and achieve greater emotional stability, interventions like exposure therapy can yield some very dramatic and rapid changes in personality traits. In exposure therapy, the therapist encourages the client to systematically confront the feared situation in order to reduce the individual's fearful reaction to the stimulus. David's therapist used a graded exposure approach in which they targeted his mildly feared situations first, followed by situations that triggered greater fears. In this way, the patient gradually builds emotional strength by tolerating higher and higher levels of discomfort. To get started, David created a list of things he worried about and ranked his worries according to the discomfort he anticipated they would cause if they came true.

## DAVID'S LIST OF WORRIES

| Feared Outcome | Worry Level (0–100) |
|---|---|
| Getting kicked out of school | 90 |
| Failing a test | 85 |
| Oversleeping and missing an exam | 80 |
| Oversleeping and missing a class | 75 |
| Not knowing an answer when called upon in class | 70 |
| Getting distracted during class and missing important information for a test | 65 |

The exposure component of the therapy can be either *in vivo*, wherein the therapist exposes the patient to the feared situation in the real world, or *imagined*, in which the patient vividly imagines the feared stimulus. Because real-world confrontations were impractical for David, his psychologist helped him imagine his feared outcomes beginning with his least feared one—becoming distracted during class.

David augmented his worry exposure therapy by spending time outside of his therapy sessions writing a "worry script." A worry script helps people face their fears directly, which helps them become less frightening.

Worry scripts can provide a clear picture of exactly what you fear. They begin with worst-case scenarios, which David had already defined with his therapist. At home, David took his list a step further by focusing on his anticipated feelings and reactions to each situation. For example, he imagined in detail what would happen if he overslept and missed a test. He wrote down the specifics of his reactions, including as many vivid and visual details as possible. David's therapist helped by reminding him that simply writing about something bad won't make it happen. Also, the goal of his worry script was not to make David stop caring about school. Instead, it helped him spend less time and energy worrying about unfounded fears.

You may decide to use some of the strategies that worked for Beth and David or one of the many other approaches currently available. Keep in mind, however, that despite your best planning efforts, you may experience some hiccups during your acting phase. The therapist you chose may not turn out to be the best fit for you. Perhaps you discover that going it alone is not cutting it and you need to find a counselor. Maybe the friend or family member who has been sabotaging your efforts to change starts influencing you again.

Two major challenges that people experience during the acting phase are (1) giving up on their initial strategy too early or (2) not shifting gears to a different approach if the first one proves to be inadequate.

The personality-change research analyzed by psychologist Brent Roberts and his coworkers at the University of Illinois indicates that for most people, the greatest incremental advances occur during the first 30 days and then plateau thereafter, but don't be discouraged if it takes you a bit longer. You may only notice minimal change during the first two weeks. However, if you reach an impasse after three weeks or find that you are getting worse, you may need to return to your planning phase and reconsider an alternate intervention strategy. If you feel that your current therapist is not helping you, then get a consultation or try a different approach. You may want to reassess your goals and consider making them more realistic or perhaps try a more aggressive approach to intervention by switching from self-help to therapy.

## STAYING THE COURSE FOR THE LONG HAUL

It took Beth almost four weeks to accomplish her initial goal of getting her boyfriend to move out and then beginning to date again. She had increased her extraversion and decreased her agreeableness, and as a result, her confidence level was much higher.

Once you have achieved the personality change you desire, your hardest work is done. No doubt you will feel even more empowered when your new behaviors become routine habits and you really have achieved your goals. But you are not completely out of the woods yet—you'll need to continue monitoring yourself to sustain your new personality traits and avoid setbacks. If something should trigger your old behaviors or thinking patterns and you do have a slip, being prepared with a plan to bounce back quickly will be crucial to your long-term success.

Beth did well in her biweekly psychotherapy sessions during her acting phase. After Ethan moved out, she started meeting new people through introductions by friends as well as internet dating sites. The cognitive behavioral therapy was helping her become more outgoing so she was more comfortable on her dates, and after about four weeks, we decided to cut back on her therapy and only meet once a week.

At the next session, Beth seemed distracted and down. When I asked what was going on, she started to cry and told me that she'd had a setback. After an unpleasant date with a guy she met on a dating site, she went home feeling discouraged and lonely. She called Ethan, who came to her rescue. They had sex, and he slept over, but the next day she regretted that she had been so weak.

I immediately shifted to a more supportive therapeutic approach and reminded Beth that slips are common. She needed to learn how to use the CPAS method as a safety net to avoid future setbacks. We revisited her planning phase, and Beth chose to come back to therapy twice a week for another few weeks until she felt stronger emotionally. I learned that she had also cut back on her CBT exercises at home and suggested that she may have done that too soon.

Beth and I explored in more detail what had triggered her slip. Her most recent date had sounded really terrific online and on the phone, and she was secretly hoping that this new guy would be the love of her life. Instead, he turned out to be completely different from what his online profile suggested, and that was a tremendous letdown for Beth. We discussed ways that Beth could refocus her thoughts on more realistic outcomes for her future dates in order to avoid another intense disappointment that might trigger another slip.

## SAFETY NET STRATEGY FOR MAINTAINING CHANGE

- *Expect setbacks.* Remember, to err is human, so forgive yourself if you slip back temporarily to your old ways.

- *Identify your triggers.* Explore the situation and feelings that set you off and made you regress to your unwanted behaviors so you can avoid them in the future.

- *Revisit your CPAS Method for Change.*
  - *Considering phase.* Review your list of self-inflicted barriers and excuses, and remind yourself why they no longer make sense.
  - *Planning phase.* Self-help may not be enough for you or you may need to change your therapy strategy or even your therapist. Also, anticipate that your triggers for slips may happen again, so have a plan in place to avoid or shorten these setbacks.
  - *Acting phase.* If you have a major slip, you may want to try a revised intervention approach.
  - *Sustaining phase.* Be ready with safety-net methods in case you need them. Make a list of all the things that are better in your life since you made a change.

As your desired personality changes become more stable during your sustaining phase, you will also benefit from becoming more *resilient*, which means you can recover more quickly from a setback. Resilience is essentially emotional and psychological elasticity. Your long-term success is not just about staying the course through adversity; it is about being able to recharge and recommit after you stumble.

Although one's capacity for resilience develops early in life, resilience researchers have shown that people can bolster their ability to rebound from setbacks throughout their lives. Studies have shown that building supportive social networks is an effective way to strengthen resilience.

You can also prepare for lapses by planning a minilapse. This is a way to remind yourself how your old behaviors made you feel bad and reassure yourself that you can quickly pull yourself back to your new and healthier lifestyle. Beth planned a minilapse wherein she stayed home by herself for a weekend. The isolation brought back her old feelings of low self-esteem, and again she felt like reaching out to Ethan for solace. Fortunately, she now had the tools (CBT homework, meditation, talk therapy) to resist.

---

### STRATEGIES FOR BUILDING RESILIENCE

- *Get support from friends.* Research indicates that strong personal and professional relationships assist people in coping with adversity. Share your goals with a supportive friend or family member who you can turn to when you need some support.

- *Stay positive.* It is possible to learn to be more optimistic. Thinking positive thoughts and spending time with optimistic people will help you recover from slips more quickly.

- *Remain objective.* We all have a tendency to judge ourselves too harshly after a setback. Remember that everyone makes mistakes. Expect them and move on without self-blame.

- *Systematically reduce stress.* Take time for meditation, exercise, or other stress-release breaks, which will help build your resilience and reduce setbacks.

- *Try planning a controlled minilapse.* Prove to yourself that you can bounce back to the new you by allowing yourself to temporarily lapse into an old behavior.

---

One of the most common reasons for a setback is everyday stress that triggers old habits. We can't completely eliminate stress from our lives, but we can learn to manage it better. Stress-reduction strategies are easy to learn and have been shown to be effective. Some stress-management methods, such as psychotherapy and mindfulness meditation, may already be part of your personality-change action plan. Managing stress more effectively will not only reduce your risk for a setback but also improve your well-being and physical health.

If you've prepared yourself properly, you will breeze through the sustaining phase, develop more confidence about your capacity to change, and perhaps even consider taking on loftier goals and changing other aspects of your personality. For some people, however, the sustaining phase can be particularly challenging because of unanticipated life events, stress, or other causes. One issue may be that your goals from the outset were unrealistic—perhaps achievable in the short run but not for the long haul.

If Beth had experienced several setbacks because of her dating experiences, she might have had to reconsider her immediate goal of beginning to date men who want to have kids. Perhaps it was enough at this point to just get used to living on her own and wait until she had more emotional strength before exposing herself to the stressors and potential triggers of the dating scene.

If you find that you are still struggling despite your best efforts to improve your resilience and bounce back from setbacks, it may be worth reconsidering your original goals and making them more realistic. Also, if you've been going it alone, you might consider getting some help from a therapist.

## ENJOYING THE NEW YOU

Bravo on your remarkable achievement—you have made real and meaningful change for the better. I expect that the process was not as daunting as you anticipated. Your new behaviors and refined personality are now a part of who you are. Despite the widely held misconception that trying to change your personality can take forever and a day, you were able to commit to change, and you probably achieved it in less time than you anticipated.

As you move forward in your life, you will likely continue to practice many of the strategies that worked for you. If you found that a counselor or therapist helped, then that person could become an ongoing resource to enlist at times of stress. Perhaps your meditation sessions were key to building your resilience and your morning meditation practice has now become a part of your daily routine.

With each passing day, new challenges will emerge, and you may find that your new personality could use some further refinement. You may wish to return to the strategies that worked for you or perhaps try a different approach for achieving new goals. Whatever happens, having already made a significant change in your life will fortify you against future difficulties so you can remain healthy, happy, and fulfilled as a new and better version of yourself.

# Bibliography

## PREFACE

Hudson, N. W., & Roberts, B. W. "Goals to change personality traits: Concurrent links between personality traits, daily behavior, and goals to change oneself." *Journal of Research in Personality* 53 (2014): 68–83.

## CHAPTER 1: PERSONALITY CAN CHANGE

Alred, A., et al. "The relationship between academic major, personality type, and stress in college students." *Eukaryon* 9 (2013): https://www.lakeforest.edu/live/files/1587-allredgrangerhogstrompdf.

American Psychiatric Association. *Diagnostic and statistical manual of mental disorders: DSM-5.* Washington, DC: American Psychiatric Association, 2013.

DeYoung, C. G., et al. "Testing predictions from personality neuroscience: Brain structure and the Big Five." *Psychological Science* 21, no. 6 (2010): 820–828.

Ellis, P. D. *The essential guide to effect sizes: Statistical power, meta-analysis, and the interpretation of research results.* 1st ed. Cambridge, UK: Cambridge University Press, 2010.

Gosling, S. D., et al. "Personalities of self-identified 'dog people' and 'cat people.'" *Anthrozoös* 23, no. 3 (2010): 213–222.

Greengross, G., & Miller, G., F. "The Big Five personality traits of professional comedians compared to amateur comedians, comedy writers, and college students." *Personality and Individual Differences* 47, no. 2 (2009): 79–83.

Hartshorne, J. K. "How birth order affects your personality." *Scientific American*. 2010: http://www.scientificamerican.com/article.cfm?id=ruled-by-birth-order.

Jang, K. L., et al. "Heritability of the Big Five personality dimensions and their facets: A twin study." *Journal of Personality* 64, no. 3 (1996): 577–591.

Judge, T. A., et al. "The Big Five personality traits, general mental ability, and career success across the life span." *Personnel Psychology* 52, no. 3 (1999): 621–652.

Krawczyk, M. W. "Probability weighting in different domains: The role of affect, fungibility, and stakes." *Journal of Economic Psychology* 51 (2015): 1–15.

Leichsenring, F. "Are psychodynamic and psychoanalytic therapies effective? A review of empirical data." *International Journal of Psychoanalysis* 86 (2005): 841–868.

Mroczek, D. K., & Spiro, A., III. "Personality change influences mortality in older men." *Psychological Science* 18 (2007): 371–376.

Nave, C. S., et al. "On the contextual independence of personality: Teachers' assessments predict directly observed behavior after four decades." *Social Psychological and Personality Science* 1, no. 4 (2010): 327–334.

Roberts, B. W., et al. "A systematic review of personality trait change through intervention." *Psychological Bulletin* 143, no. 2 (2017): 117–141.

Rohrer, J. M., et al. "Examining the effects of birth order on personality." *Proceedings of the National Academy of Sciences U.S.A.* 112, no. 46 (2015): 14224–14229.

Ryckman, R. M. *Theories of Personality.* 10th ed. Independence, KY: Cengage Advantage Books, 2012.

Turiano, N. A., et al. "Personality trait level and change as predictors of health outcomes: Findings from a national study of Americans (MIDUS)." *Journal of Gerontology* 67, no. 1 (2012): 4–12.

Wang, H.-X., et al. "Personality and lifestyle in relation to dementia incidence." *Neurology* 72 (2009): 253–259.

## CHAPTER 2: FOUR PHASES OF CHANGE

Aral, S., & Nicolaides C. "Exercise contagion in a global social network." *Nature Communications* 8, no. 14753 (2017). doi:10.1038/ncomms14753.

Graybiel, A. M., & Smith, K. S. "Good habits, bad habits." *Scientific American.* June 2015: 39–43.

Moore, M., et al. "Coaching behavior change." Available online: https://pdfs.semanticscholar.org/77c0/4815e762541b7b0e8 986dfdcf26277a9732f.pdf.

Prochaska, J. O., et al. "Stages of change and decisional balance for 12 problem behaviors." *Health Psychology* 18, no. 1 (1994): 39–46.

## CHAPTER 3: ASSESS YOURSELF AND DEFINE YOUR GOALS

Jason, D. "The utter uselessness of job interviews." *New York Times.* April 8, 2017: https://www.nytimes.com/2017/04/08/opinion/sunday/the-utter-uselessness-of-job-interviews.html?_r=0.

John, O. P., et al. "Paradigm shift to the integrative big-five trait taxonomy: History, measurement, and conceptual issues." In John, O. P., et al. (Eds.), *Handbook of personality: Theory and research*, 114–158. New York, NY: Guilford Press, 2008.

McCabe, K. O., & Fleeson, W. "Are traits useful? Explaining trait manifestations as tools in pursuit of goals." *Journal of Personality and Social Psychology* 110, no. 2 (2016): 287–301.

Rammstedt, B., & John, O. P. "Measuring personality in one minute or less: A 10-item short version of the Big Five Inventory in English and German." *Journal of Research in Personality* 41 (2007): 203–212.

## CHAPTER 4: EXTRAVERSION 101

Cain, S. *Quiet: The power of introverts in a world that can't stop talking*. New York, NY: Broadway Books, 2013.

Cohen, M. X., et al. "Individual differences in extraversion and dopamine genetics predict neural reward responses." *Brain Research. Cognitive Brain Research* 25, no. 3 (2005): 851–861.

Glinski, K., & Page, A. C. "Modifiability of neuroticism, extraversion, and agreeableness by group cognitive behaviour therapy for social anxiety disorder." *Behaviour Change* 27, no. 1 (2010): 42–52.

Holmes, A. J., et al. "Individual differences in amygdala-medial prefrontal anatomy link negative affect, impaired social functioning, and polygenic depression risk." *Journal of Neuroscience* 32, no. 50 (2012): 18087–18100.

Holt-Lunstad, J., et al. "Social relationships and mortality risk: A meta-analytic review." *PLoS Medicine* 7, no. 7 (2010): e1000316. doi: 10.1371/journal.pmed.1000316.

Sugiura, M., et al. "Correlation between human personality and neural activity in cerebral cortex." *NeuroImage* 11, no. 5 (2000): 541–546.

Umberson, D., & Montez, J. K. "Social relationships and health: A flashpoint for health policy." *Journal of Health and Social Behavior* 51, Suppl. (2010): S54–S66.

## CHAPTER 5: BECOMING MORE CONSCIENTIOUS

Berchicci, M., et al. "Benefits of physical exercise on the aging brain: The role of the prefrontal cortex." *Journal of Gerontology, Series A: Biological Sciences and Medical Sciences* 68, no. 11 (2013): 1337–1341.

Chiao, C. Y., & Hsiao C. Y. "Comparison of personality traits and successful aging in older Taiwanese." *Geriatrics & Gerontology International* (May 10, 2017). doi: 10.1111/ggi.13019. [Epub ahead of print].

Higgins, D. M., et al. "Prefrontal cognitive ability, intelligence, Big Five personality and the prediction of advanced academic and workplace performance." *Journal of Personality and Social Psychology* 93, no. 2 (2007): 298–319.

Hirsh, J. B., et al. "Metatraits of the Big Five differentially predict engagement and restraint of behavior." *Journal of Personality* 77, no. 4 (2009): 1085–1101.

Jackson, J., et al. "Exploring the relationship between personality and regional brain volume in healthy aging." *Neurobiology of Aging* 32, no. 12 (2011): 2162–2171.

Kohn, M. L., & Schooler, C. "Job conditions and personality: A longitudinal assessment of their reciprocal effects." *American Journal of Sociology* 87, no. 6 (1982): 1257–1286.

Modesto-Lowe, V., et al. "Does mindfulness meditation improve attention in attention deficit hyperactivity disorder?" *World Journal of Psychiatry* 22, no. 5 (2015): 397–403.

Peterson, S. J., & Smith, G. T. "Association between elementary school personality and high school smoking and drinking." *Addiction* (June 10, 2017). doi: 10.1111/add.13905. [Epub ahead of print].

Ralph, B. C. W., et al. "Wandering minds and wavering goals: Examining the relation between mind wandering and grit in everyday life and the classroom." *Canadian Journal of Experimental Psychology* 71, no. 2 (2017): 120–132.

Rentfrow, P. J., et al. "A theory of the emergence, persistence, and expression of geographic variation in psychological characteristics." *Perspectives on Psychological Science* 3, no. 5 (2008): 339–369.

Roberts, B. W., et al. "Chapter 25: Conscientiousness." In Leary, M. R. & Hoyle, R. H. (Eds.), *Handbook of individual differences in social behavior*, 257–273. New York: Guilford Press, 2007.

Signal, T. L., et al. "Scheduled napping as a countermeasure to sleepiness in air traffic controllers." *Journal of Sleep Research* 18, no. 1 (2009): 11–19. doi: 10.1111/j.1365-2869.2008.00702.x.

Sofis, M., J., et al. "Maintained physical activity induced changes in delay discounting." *Behavior Modification* 41, no. 4 (2017): 499–528.

## CHAPTER 6: LEARNING TO AGREE

aan het Rot, M., et al. "Social behaviour and mood in everyday life: The effects of tryptophan in quarrelsome individuals." *Journal of Psychiatry & Neuroscience* 31, no. 4 (2006): 253–262.

Ashton, M. C., et al. "Kin altruism, reciprocal altruism, and the Big Five personality factors." *Evolution and Human Behavior* 19 (1998): 243–255.

Bresin, K., & Robinson, M. D. "You are what you see and choose: Agreeableness and situation selection." *Journal of Personality* 83, no. 4 (2015): 452–463.

Castle, E., et al. "Neural and behavioral bases of age differences in perceptions of trust." *Proceedings of the National Academy of Sciences U.S.A.* 109, no. 51 (2012): 20848–20852.

Davidson, R. J., et al. "Alterations in brain and immune function produced by mindfulness meditation." *Psychosomatic Medicine* 65, no. 4 (2003): 564–570.

de Haan, A., et al. "Longitudinal impact of parental and adolescent personality on parenting." *Journal of Personality and Social Psychology* 102, no. 1 (2012): 189–199.

Feingold, A. "Gender differences in personality: A meta-analysis." *Psychological Bulletin* 116, no. 3 (1994): 429–456.

Fleeson, W., et al. "An intraindividual process approach to the relationship between extraversion and positive affect: Is acting extraverted as 'good' as being extraverted?" *Journal of Personality and Social Psychology* 82, no. 6 (2002): 1409–1422.

Glass, T. A., et al. "Population based study of social and productive activities as predictors of survival among elderly Americans." *British Medical Journal* 319 (1999): 478–483.

Hurtz, G. M., & Donovan, J. J. "Personality and job performance: The Big Five revisited." *Journal of Applied Psychology* 85 (2000): 869–879.

Jang, K. L., et al. "Heritability of the Big Five personality dimensions and their facets: A twin study." *Journal of Personality* 64, no. 3 (1996): 577–591.

Judge, T., et al. "Do nice guys—and gals—really finish last? The joint effects of sex and agreeableness on income." *Journal of Personality and Social Psychology* 102, no. 2 (2012): 390–407.

Karlin, W. A., et al. "Workplace social support and ambulatory cardiovascular activity in New York City traffic agents." *Psychosomatic Medicine* 65 (2003): 167–176.

Kelley, J. M., et al. "Patient and practitioner influences on the placebo effect in irritable bowel syndrome." *Psychosomatic Medicine* 71, no. 7 (2009): 789–797.

Luo, X., et al. "Personality traits of agreeableness and extraversion are associated with ADH4 variation." *Biological Psychiatry* 61, no. 5 (2007): 599–608.

McCrae, R. R., & Costa, P. T. "The NEO Personality Inventory: Using the five-factor model in counseling." *Journal of Counseling and Development* (1991). doi: 10.1002/j.1556-6676.1991. tb01524.

McCullough, M. E. "Forgiveness: Who does it and how do they do it?" *Current Directions in Psychological Science* 10, no. 6 (2001): 194–197.

Mkoji, D., & Sikalieh, D. "The influence of personality dimensions on organizational performance." *International Journal of Humanities and Social Science* 2, no. 17 (2012): 184–194.

Organ, D. W., & Lingl, A. "Personality, satisfaction, and organizational citizenship behavior." *Journal of Social Psychology* 135, no. 3 (1995): 339–350.

Rowe, J. W., & Kahn, R. L. *Successful aging.* New York: Dell, 1999.

Segerstrom, S. C., & Sephton, S. E. "Optimistic expectancies and cell-mediated immunity: The role of positive affect." *Psychological Science* 21, no. 3 (2010): 448–455.

Soto, C. J. "Is happiness good for your personality? Concurrent and prospective relations of the Big Five with subjective well-being." *Journal of Personality* 83, no. 1 (2015): 45–55.

Singer, T., et al. "Empathy for pain involves the affective but not sensory components of pain." *Science* 303 (2004): 1157–1162.

Sutin, A., et al. "Personality and obesity across the adult life span." *Journal of Personality and Social Psychology* 101, no. 3 (2011): 579–592.

Terracciano, A., et al. "Genome-wide association scan for five major dimensions of personality." *Molecular Psychiatry* 15, no. 6 (2010): 647–656.

Winston, J. S., et al. "Automatic and intentional brain responses during evaluation of trustworthiness of faces." *Nature Neuroscience* 5, no. 3 (2002): 277–283.

## CHAPTER 7: TAMING YOUR NEUROSIS

Allen, B., & Lauterbach, D. "Personality characteristics of adult survivors of childhood trauma." *Journal of Traumatic Stress* 20 (2007): 587–595.

Andersson, G., et al. "Internet-based psychodynamic versus cognitive behavioral guided self-help for generalized anxiety disorder: A randomized controlled trial." *Psychotherapy and Psychosomatics* 81 (2012): 344–355.

Blumenthal, J. A., et al. "Is exercise a viable treatment for depression?" *American College of Sports Medicine's Health & Fitness Journal* 16, no. 4 (2012): 14–21.

Coplan, J. D., et al. "The relationship between intelligence and anxiety: An association with subcortical white matter metabolism." *Frontiers in Evolutionary Neuroscience* 3, no. 8 (2012). doi: 10.3389/fnevo.2011.00008. eCollection 2011.

Gurtman, C. G., et al. "The role of neuroticism in insomnia." *Clinical Psychologist* 18 (2014): 116–124.

Hoyer, J., et al. "Worry exposure versus applied relaxation in the treatment of generalized anxiety disorder." *Psychotherapy and Psychosomatics* 78 (2009): 106–115.

Johnson, A. B., et al. "Accurately diagnosing and treating borderline personality disorder: A psychotherapeutic case." *Psychiatry* 7, no. 4 (2010): 21–30.

Lahey, B. "Public health significance of neuroticism." *American Psychologist* 64, no. 4 (2009): 241–256.

Paxling, B., et al. "Guided internet-delivered cognitive behavior therapy for generalized anxiety disorder: A Randomized controlled trial." *Cognitive Behaviour Therapy* 40, no. 3 (2011): 159–173.

Roberts, B. W., et al. "Chapter 25: Conscientiousness." In Leary, M. R., & Hoyle, R. H. (Eds.), *Handbook of individual differences in social behavior*, 257–273. New York: Guilford Press, 2007.

Sareen, J., et al. "The relationship between anxiety disorders and physical disorders in the U.S. National Comorbidity Survey." *Depression and Anxiety* 21 (2005): 193–202.

Servaas, M. N., et al. "Neuroticism and the brain: A quantitative meta-analysis of neuroimaging studies investigating emotion processing." *Neuroscience & Biobehavioral Reviews* 8 (2013): 1518–1529.

Turiano, N. A., et al. "Big 5 personality traits and interleukin-6: Evidence for 'healthy neuroticism' in a US population sample." *Brain, Behavior, and Immunity* 28 (2013): 83–89.

Van der Heiden, C., & ten Broeke, E. "The when, why, and how of worry exposure." *Cognitive and Behavioral Practice* 16 (2009): 386–393.

## CHAPTER 8: OPENING UP TO NEW EXPERIENCES

Boyce, C. J., et al. "Personality change following unemployment." *Journal of Applied Psychology* 100, no. 4 (2015): 991–1011.

Cimarelli, G., et al. "Dog owners' interaction styles: Their components and associations with reactions of pet dogs to a social threat." *Frontiers in Psychology* 7, no. 1979 (2016). doi: 10.3389/fpsyg.2016.01979. eCollection 2016.

Costa, P. T., et al. "Cross-sectional studies of personality in a national sample: 2. Stability in neuroticism, extraversion, and openness." *Psychology and Aging* 1, no. 2 (1986): 144–149.

de Haan, A. D., et al. "Longitudinal impact of parental and adolescent personality on parenting." *Journal of Personality and Social Psychology* 102 (2012): 189–199.

DeYoung, C. G., et al. "Sources of openness/intellect: Cognitive and neuropsychological correlates of the fifth factor of personality." *Journal of Personality* 73, no. 4 (2005): 825–858.

Feist, G. J. "A meta-analysis of the impact of personality on scientific and artistic creativity." *Personality and Social Psychological Review* 2 (1998): 290–309.

Jang, K. L., et al. "Heritability of the Big Five personality dimensions and their facets: A twin study." *Journal of Personality* 64, no. 3 (1996): 577–592.

Joinson, C., & Nettle, D. "Season of birth variation in sensation seeking in an adult population." *Personality and Individual Differences* 38, no. 4 (2005): 859–870.

Kochanska, G., et al. "Parents' personality and infants' temperament as contributors to their emerging relationship." *Journal of Personality and Social Psychology* 86, no. 5 (2014): 744–759.

Kosinski, M., et al. "Private traits and attributes are predictable from digital records of human behavior." *Proceedings of the National Academy of Sciences U.S.A.* 110, no. 15 (2013): 5802–5805.

Malouff, J. M., et al. "The relationship between the five-factor model of personality and symptoms of clinical disorders: A meta-analysis." *Journal of Psychopathology and Behavioral Assessment* 27, no. 2 (2005): 101–114.

McCrae, R. R. "Openness to experience: Expanding the boundaries of Factor V." *European Journal of Personality* 8, no. 4 (1994): 251–272.

McCrae, R. R., & Costa, P. T. "Validation of the five-factor model of personality across instruments and observers." *Journal of Personality and Social Psychology* 52, no. 1 (1987): 81–90.

Piedmont, R., et al. "Using the five-factor model to identify a new personality disorder domain: The case for experiential permeability." *Journal of Personality and Social Psychology* 96, no. 6 (2009): 1245–1258.

Rentfrow, P. J., et al. "A theory of the emergence, persistence, and expression of geographic variation in psychological characteristics." *Perspectives on Psychological Science* 3, no. 5 (2008): 339–369.

Riccelli, R., et al. "Surface-based morphometry reveals the neuroanatomical basis of the five-factor model of personality." *Social Cognitive and Affective Neuroscience* 12, no. 4 (2017): 671–684.

Schmitt, R., et al. "Why can't a man be more like a woman? Sex differences in Big Five personality traits across 55 cultures." *Journal of Personality and Social Psychology* 94, no. 1 (2008): 168–182.

Schretlen, D. J., et al. "A neuropsychological study of personality: Trait openness in relation to intelligence, fluency, and executive functioning." *Journal of Clinical and Experimental Neuropsychology* 32, no. 10 (2010): 1068–1073.

Stephan, Y. "Openness to experience and active older adults' life satisfaction: A trait and facet-level analysis." *Personality and Individual Differences* 47, no. 6 (2009): 637–641.

Volkow, N. D., et al. "Adverse health effects of marijuana use." *New England Journal of Medicine* 370, no. 23 (2014): 2219–2227.

Weisberg, Y. J., et al. "Gender differences in personality across the ten aspects of the Big Five." *Frontiers in Psychology* (2011): https://doi.org/10.3389/fpsyg.2011.00178.

White-Schwoch, T., et al. "Older adults benefit from music training early in life: Biological evidence for long-term training-driven plasticity." *Journal of Neuroscience* 33, no. 45 (2013): 17667–17674.

Zhang, Y., et al. "Relationship between hypnosis and personality trait in participants with high or low hypnotic susceptibility." *Neuropsychiatric Disease and Treatment* 13 (2017): 1007–1012.

## CHAPTER 9: FAST-TRACKING YOUR CHANGE WITH THERAPY

Anderson, T., et al. "Therapist effects: Facilitative interpersonal skills as a predictor of therapist success." *Journal of Clinical Psychology* 65 (2009): 755–768.

Lutz, W., et al. "Therapist effects in outpatient psychotherapy: A three-level growth curve approach." *Journal of Counseling Psychology* 54 (2007): 32–39.

Miller, B. F., et al. "Proximity of providers: Colocating behavioral health and primary care and the prospects for an integrated workforce." *American Psychologist* 69, no. 4 (2014): 443–451.

Roberts, B. W., et al. "A systematic review of personality trait change through intervention." *Psychological Bulletin* 143, no. 2 (2017): 117–141.

Zarbo, C., et al. "Integrative psychotherapy works." *Frontiers in Psychiatry* 6, no. 2021 (2016). doi: 10.3389/fpsyg.2015.02021. eCollection 2015.

## CHAPTER 10: 30 DAYS TO A BETTER YOU

Aldrich, D. P., & Kyota, E. "Creating community resilience through elder-led physical and social infrastructure." *Disaster Medicine and Public Health Preparedness* 11, no. 1 (2017): 120–126.

Bakker, D., et al. "Mental health smartphone apps: Review and evidence-based recommendations for future developments." *Journal of Medical Internet Research Mental Health* 3, no. 1 (2016): e7. doi: 10.2196/mental.4984.

Foa, E. B., et al. "Randomized trial of prolonged exposure for post-traumatic stress disorder with and without cognitive restructuring: Outcome at academic and community clinics." *Journal of Consulting and Clinical Psychology* 73 (2005): 953–964.

Goyal, M., et al. "Meditation programs for psychological stress and well-being: A systematic review and meta-analysis." *Journal of the American Medical Association Internal Medicine* 174 (2014): 357–368.

Johansson, R., et al. "Using the internet to provide psychodynamic psychotherapy." *Psychodynamic Psychiatry* 41, no. 4 (2013): 513–540.

Lavretsky, L. *Resilience and aging: Research and practice.* 1st ed. Baltimore, MD: Johns Hopkins University Press, 2014.

McKenna, K. M., et al. "The missing link: Connection is the key to resilience in medical education." *Academic Medicine* 92, no. 9 (2016): 1197–1199.

Ost, L. G., et al. "One vs five sessions of exposure and five sessions of cognitive therapy in the treatment of claustrophobia." *Behavior Research and Therapy* 39 (2001): 167–183.

Prayson, R. A., et al. "Medical student resilience strategies: A content analysis of medical students' portfolios." *Perspectives in Medical Education* 6, no 1 (2017): 29–35.

Roberts, B. W., et al. "A systematic review of personality trait change through intervention." *Psychological Bulletin* 143, no. 2 (2017): 117–141.

Thoits, P. A. "Stress and health: Major findings and policy implications." *Journal of Health and Social Behavior* 51, Suppl. (2010): S41–S53.

# Index

Page numbers followed by *f* and *t* refer to figures and tables, respectively.

unemployment, 120

Watson, John, 4
wellness. *See* health,
    physical
word association tests, 41
worry, 106

worry exposure therapy, 106,
    108, 161–62

yoga, 114

Zoloft, 72